"Marcus has been through the shit and has come out of it with some wisdom, wit, his teeth, good stories and he's a less shitty person for the most part. The struggle continues. He embraces it."

—Marc Maron
comedian, author, actor

"Who the fuck comes of age with hookers, coke, and broken-down suitcase Jews? I love reading Marcus. He's the Yiddish Coltrane, weaving dirty words like blue jazz notes over paper."

—Jack Grisham
musician, author

"*#1 Son and Other Stories,* the new collection by Michael Marcus, is the kind of riveting, depraved, violent saga that makes you wonder, not just at the author's talent, but at the fact that he survived to write at all. Imagine *The Sopranos* re-fashioned as *The Shapiros* and you get the picture. Not for the faint of heart, but fans of bent memoir and balls-to-the wall writing will not be disappointed. Marcus is a true original."

—Jerry Stahl
author, screenwriter

"Michael Marcus writes with the lyrical madness of a man possessed. Or should I say a child dispossessed. His words are a gift from his mother and father, from you and me. Through the weary torture of his smashed innocence he writes with profound detail and, most importantly, with humor. His shattered abyss made beautiful."

—Malcolm Venville
director, photographer

#1 SON

AND OTHER STORIES

MICHAEL MARCUS

PUNK HOSTAGE PRESS

#1 Son and Other Stories
by Michael Marcus
© 2017 Michael Marcus, all rights reserved.

Edited by Iris Berry and Wyatt Doyle

Designed by Wyatt Doyle
Cover photo courtesy of New York State's Finest
Title illustration by Jimmy Angelina / JimmyAngelina.com

ISBN 978-0-9996141-8-1

Printed in the United States of America.

Punk Hostage Press // Hollywood, California
www.punkhostagepress.com

CONTENTS

INTRODUCTION
by Jon Hess

In each of his stories, Michael Marcus takes us on a wild adventure through the darkest depths of addiction, sexuality, deceit, and depravity with a raw grace and eloquence that brings to mind the voices of Jim Carroll in *The Basketball Diaries*, Irvine Welsh in *Trainspotting*, Denis Johnson in *Jesus' Son*, and Junot Diaz in *Drown*. Not for a moment do we question our narrator's truth as he depicts larger-than-life characters who are in a constant struggle to survive.

The details of every scene are vivid and compelling. Each and every character that Marcus has chosen to depict is unforgettable, whether it be Leo, the one-legged film lab manager, or his brutal father—who you abhor, love and respect in the context of this world of "fuck or be fucked." Never for a moment do we doubt that Carl "Dad" Marcus, this monster of a father, loves his son Michael.

Marcus has an engaging voice as an author that is matched by his raucous humor. To fully enjoy this book, take your time, read it out loud—if only to yourself. The prose is poetic. In the midst of felonious actions and cruelty to one another, the folks who inhabit this extraordinary book are ever persistent in their need to love and be loved. The absence of love and trust is a pain that our narrator survived in flamboyant fashion by self-medicating with every drug imaginable.

There is the sense that Marcus, who tells us his stories in

the first person, is a seeker of peace and serenity even as he struggles to make ends meet in his own private hell. There is a compassionate understanding that Marcus has as a storyteller, for every character in this book that resonates with the reader.

To read *#1 Son* is an experience of monumental portions. A powerful, fresh new voice has taken center stage on the literary scene.

"There are two types of people in the world, kid:
The fuckee and the fucker.
Which one you gonna be?"

—Carl Marcus

GOING FOR A DRIVE

Motoring up the 101, he pointed to the north and said, "See that area there? That's where all the lowlifes live." Then, pointing towards the beach, he said, "That's where all the winners live, kids."

"What are lowlifes, Dad?"

"Scumbags!" He shouted. "Columns of human waste. They live in clapboard houses, or, if they're lucky, stucco shitholes with screaming, schmucky kids! They work dead-end jobs with fat wives and 30-year mortgages and 5-year car notes. They have pension plans and punch a fucking clock all day. Just plain *schnorrers*."

"What's a pension, Daddy?" My sister asked.

"Baby Lorraine, it's when assholes work year after year for twenty or thirty years, and in the end they only gets a little bullshit stipends."

"What's a *schnorrer*, Daddy?"

"Mikey, it's men or women who freeload and sponge like leeches at corporate or government jobs because they have no original thoughts, business sense, or ambitions. AND EVEN WORSE, they have no panache or hustle. You never want to get caught up in that garbage, kid. It's a dead-end life. A real fucking horror show."

"OK, Dad."

He turned up Frank Sinatra and ran his gold rings on the Caddie's plastic steering wheel. He sang "My Way" as he gunned the red Eldorado up the 101 past Cambria.

My father drove us all over California. We motored from Point Conception to the Mexican border, from San Fernando to San Francisco, Burbank to Barstow and all the nooks and crannies in-between. He feed us Ghirardelli chocolates, Pismo Beach clam chowder, date shakes from Hadley's, root beer floats from A&W, fried shrimp from Howard Johnson's, and pea soup from Andersen's. On many occasions he would wad up the check and stick it in his pocket, and we'd just walk out. *Let's play a game kids. It's called dine and dash....*" If the waitress ever stopped us on the way out, he'd say, "Must have slipped my mind," then pay the bill.

Once in our travels, my father took us to Fedco. He had acquired PAID stickers that a manager friend stole from the cash register. These stickers were used for big-ticket items that couldn't be bagged. He'd slap a sticker on an item (toasters, irons, roller-skates, bicycles, even a color TV he put on a dolly) and we'd walk out.

When he was tired, he'd pull into a rest stop and say, "OK you little cuties, shut the fuck up now. I'm sleeping, and I want silence." He had no problem throwing an open fist into the backseat if we woke him. He called it "backhand therapy." At home, he called it "wall-to-wall counseling." My sister and I would sit back there, wired on sugar, and freak out about waking him. Then he'd wake up, and we were off. We also played road games.

"Hey kids, you want to play House of Horrors?"

There was silence.

"How do you play that game, Daddy?" My sister asked.

"We think of the worst possible scenario that could occur in a house filled with children."

More silence, for what seemed like eternity.

"For example, a banister that is sharpened like a shaving razor, and when you slide down it cuts you in two, ha ha!"

"OK Dad," I said nervously.

"Or a special well-lit room where they take a hole punch to your eyelids so your pupils are always exposed to the bright lights."

"Eww," said Lorraine.

"Or a chair with tacks and nails on it that you're forced to sit in."

"Dad, how about being stuck in a car that plays Frank Sinatra, over and over and over, forever?"

"Ha, ha smartass. No, no Sinatra is not in this game, he's a musical genius. That faggot Liberace is a different story."

"What's a faggot, Daddy?"

"Michael, that's men who suck each others cocks and screw each other's buttholes."

"Eww," my sister and me replied in unison.

"Run away from any man that wants you to do that to him—or even worse, wants to do it to you."

"Dad, has that ever happened to you?"

"NO! As a matter of fact, a man approached me when I was about your age, Michael. He went to touch me on the shoulder; I punched him square in the balls."

"Ha," we laughed.

"Well, it turned out to be the next-door neighbor just making a friendly gesture. But better safe than sorry."

"Did you apologize, Daddy?"

"No, Lorraine. I never apologize for shit! Fuck that!"

"Really, Dad, not for anything?"

"Michael, it is a sign of regret, of weakness. I mean unless it's really something awful. Otherwise, fuck 'em."

"Oh, OK Daddy."

"Listen you two, their are two types of people in this world."

"Girls and boys, right, Dad?" I asked.

"White people and black people, right, Daddy?" Lorraine said.

"No, no, you little cuties!"

"Well what then, Dad?"

"Michael, Lorraine: There is the *fuckee* and the *fucker*, which one are you gonna be?"

"What's the difference? They're both dirty words?"

"Yeah Daddy, I don't wanna be either one," I added.

"*Mehhh!* Wrong! I'm talking about don't let anybody take advantage of you! Fuck 'em first—you understand, kids? Fuck 'em first."

And it was those three words that shaped the next 30 years of my life.

As he cranked up Sinatra's "New York, New York," we cruised the Caddy through San Simeon, up the California coast.

DAD'S WAY

I should probably preface this story by saying that my father is a very violent man.

I'm in a theatre with my father, watching *Jaws*. We're at a matinee in Palm Springs. My dad let me play hooky occasionally, when he was bored. My father chain-smoked Tareyton 100's, Everyone chain-smoked. The theater is smoky, like a pool hall.

About an hour into the film, a man is walking back and forth in our row. He's lost a wallet, or keys, something important. Then he left. Now he's back. He's borrowed a flashlight from the usher and is searching the aisles quite frantically. In his search, the flashlight's beam hits my father's eyes.

"Get that fucking light out of my eyes," my father growls.

"I'm looking for something," he says.

"I'm trying to watch a movie with my kid, guy. Don't fuck us around."

"I said I'm looking for something, asshole."

"Uh oh," I say.

Then my father: "Whad'ja call me, you fuck?"

I'm pretending not to be there. I'm pretending this isn't happening.

Just a couple of months before, at a bar called Blackbeard's in Newport Beach, my father was trying to pick up a girl. A man came up and asked my father, "What happened to your face? Did someone cut you, man?"

I was in earshot of this, playing Pong. I knew. I just knew this was going to be bad. My father had cystic acne and his face was scarred badly. The woman he was trying to pick up went to say something; my father put his left hand up to her face and simultaneously with his right hand picked up a heavy vodka glass. In one snapping motion, he hit the man in the face with it. It broke with a clinging, chattering sound on the bridge of the man's nose and upper lip and gum area. The man put booth hands over his face and I laughed, because it reminded me of a game I played with my baby cousin. He fell to his knees, and my father kicked him a couple of times, yelling, *What happened to your face, man? What happened to your face?"*

Dad grabbed me by the nape of my shirt and we ran outta there before Newport's finest arrived. Later that night he turned himself in, and paid a lot of money to not go to jail. He ended up paying the medical bills for a man who asked the wrong question to the wrong man at the wrong time.

These thoughts were broken by the current situation. "You heard me, asshole, I called you an asshole." As he says this, he is waving the flashlight in my father's eyes, instigating his own demise.

In one very quick movement, my father is out of his seat, grabbing the guy by the collar and pulling him up to his height. They are face-to-face now. My father says something in a hushed tone. I can't hear what he was saying, and I couldn't see what was going on. But then the guy screamed, a high-pitched scream. On the big screen, Roy Scheider is throwing fish, chumming the water for sharks. The flashlight guy is whimpering like a baby, now sitting in a theatre seat. My father is standing over him, saying, *"Now who's the asshole, huh? Now who?"*

The house lights go on. I look over at the guy. My father had bit him, and his cheek is like a flap, flapping in the wind of my father's scorn and ridicule. Then my father does the second most unpredictable thing: Reaches into his pocket, pulls out a wad—I mean like a couple of thousand dollars—peels off three or four one hundred dollar bills, throws them at the guy and says, "Go fix yourself, scumbag."

"You animal," the man whimpers.

We leave the theatre and drive home in silence, which is broken by my dad.

"You hungry, Mikey? You wanna eat at Sizzler?"

Too nauseous to eat but too scared to say no, I reply, "Sure, Dad."

THIEVIN' PINK PILLS AND PSYCHOTROPIC THRILLS

Jeff was an orderly at the state mental hospital in Camarillo. He often told me stories of the "hot" mental patients he had sex with, and constantly mentioned medications he stole from the hospital. I would bump into him at the Sunday Bagel Brunch, sponsored by Western Bagel. This event took place at the Oakwood Garden Apartments hospitality room. The room was always packed. It seemed like every resident would show up for free bagels, Danish, orange juice and coffee. I'd go in hung over or high, cutting in front of people, getting yelled at by all the *alter cockers*, who would often show up in robes or nightgowns. I would hit it hard, often getting three or four plates of bagels, lox, Danish, and donuts.

I was a pushy, rude-ass little punk who didn't give a fuck. I loved to get fucked up, steal shit, and fuck girls. And I loved to eat. "You eat like you have two assholes," my step-father would say.

I brought a pint of Stoli to mix with the OJ. I was milling about when I saw Jeff.

"Hey, Jeff."

He didn't hear me.

"JEFF!" I yelled.

He was flirting with a 65-year-old divorcee named Sunny Goldstein. She was always tanning. Everybody in the complex constantly told her how young she looked. She had fake tits and wore Fiorucci sunglasses, tiny bikinis, and big hats. She had tan sagging cellulite around her inner thighs and ass. She was a young spirit in a really old container.

She sauntered into the room like she was Lauren Hutton. She had cruised me by the pool a couple of times and invited me up for dinner. I imagined her pussy looked like an old catcher's mitt, and I just didn't wanna play ball. Jeff did, he was creepy that way. He had banged out a couple of old broads from the Geritol set. He couldn't seem to score with the younger chicks here.

"Yeah, hey Mike, how's it going guy?" He pulled off his Vuarnet sunglasses. I wanted those. He was wearing big, droopy surf trunks, blown-out flip-flops and a *Frampton Comes Alive* T-shirt. He also had on puka shells, though he'd never been to Hawaii, or any island, and from what I know, never went to the beach.

He had that benzodiazepine gleam (he took a lot of Valium) and a slow eye due to a congenital ocular muscle problem. He said it embarrassed his mom and dad, so they made him wear dark glasses early as a kid. He could look at the buffet table over to his left, and directly at me standing in front of him, all at the same time.

"Anything happening? Got something?" I whispered. "I need drugs."

"No, man, just psych meds, the 'zines: Stela, Thora and Compa." His speech was strained, like there was a smaller voice in the back of his throat that's trying to speak above his current voice. "Psychotropics, not the tropics I want to summer in," he laughed. A Camarillo Hospital joke I'd heard over and over. I forced a chuckle.

"Yeah, me either. I hate those things, they make me feel like that slack-jaw grandpa eating that poppy-seed bagel over there in the corner. Fucking cream cheese and lox dripping on his Rolex."

Jeff looked around and laughed. He leaned in. "Yeah, I'm going home to Santa Fe in a week. I'll bring something back. Friend of mine deals crank and coke out there." He bit into his everything bagel.

"Really? When you leaving, Jeff?" I looked over at Bunny; she winked at me. My stomach turned. *Maybe she'd pay me to fuck her...?*

"Monday night, why?" He said, dropping his head back and spitting pieces of the everything bagel into the air.

"Oh, I thought maybe we'd catch that Raiders game." Lie. I hated sports, but I loved gambling on sporting events. "No. I guess not. Well, see ya later." He walked back to Sunny. She looked past him and right at me, licking her lips. *Maybe she'd pay me to suck my dick while I look at a* Hustler *magazine?* I took a swig of vodka and OJ.

"Yeah, later Jeff." My mind was going, I had a plan.

Monday night, Jeff's apartment, Q-107, 11:30 PM. I was pacing back and forth because I couldn't get the patio sliding door off of its tracks; it usually wasn't a problem. *How the fuck...?* I had to get in. *What do I do now?* I knew Jeff kept an English cookie tin of pills in his studio apartment, he'd showed it to me a couple of weeks ago. I needed to steal it; I needed to get high. I needed to throw the ultra-heavy little hibachi through the sliding glass door: *Crash! Slam! Chinkle, chinkle, chinkle....*

I rushed into the apartment. There was briquette dust in the air and all over the floor. He had concert posters and *Playboy* centerfolds taped to the walls: Hendrix, Mott the Hoople, Humble Pie...complete with black lights. The floor was strewn with dirty socks and underwear. The coffee table had paper plates with food still on them from the weekend, along with an open container of Vaseline and *Swedish Erotica* porno vids.

I searched under the bed: No.

The closet: No.

The bathroom: No.

The refrigerator: Yep! The cookie tin was in there and

loaded with pills. So many colors and designs! I grabbed an Alpha Beta paper bag, throw the tin in the bag and walked out the front door.

I quickly walked to the exit of the building. I ducked inside a doorway. I saw the little Oakwood security cart hum by, the guard looking like business as usual. No sense of urgency, just making his rounds. I was in and out in probably two-and-a-half or three minutes. Oakwood has twenty-six buildings, lettered A through Z, three floors each. Five guys handled all the security, two vehicles. Easy pickings.

I quickly headed to P-304, Mike Anderson's apartment. Mike was my partner in crime. I knocked. No answer. Where is he?

"Mike, its Mike, come on!" I heard him creep towards the door. He looked through the peephole. He opened the door. He looked wired as fuck.

"Hey, how'd it work out? You took the whole thing? Fuck's that dirt on your face? Camouflage? Good idea! Nobody saw you come up here, right?" He chirped rapid-fire at me. Paranoid.

"Right, man. Nobody saw. Jeff's gone for a week."

"Cool. Hey, before we start taking any of these, shouldn't we find out what they are?" He asked me nervously.

"My mom's a nurse," I assured him. "She keeps a *Physician's Desk Reference* in the apartment. I'm gonna run and grab it. Don't take anything until I get back, dude!"

"Wow—look at this pink pill, this must be an elephant immobilizer."

"Hey, Mike—don't fuck around with it until I get the book."

I went back home and into the apartment where my family lived, E-302. I grabbed the *PDR*, double-timed it back to his apartment in 15 or 20 minutes, and pounded on the door. I knock and knock. No answer. Shit. This asshole couldn't wait for me? I went to the roof access and dropped down on his balcony—no hibachi needed. The door was wide open. Mike lay in a catatonic state on the floor in front of the television, staring at the ceiling. The Camel cigarette in his left hand was burned right down and through his fingers. *That's gonna hurt in the morning*—if there was a morning for him.

"Mike! Mike! Miiiiike!!!"

No answer from the pile on the ground. The cookie tin was open, pills strewn about the floor, everywhere. His lips were pink, like he'd applied lip gloss.

"What did you take?"

"Thaaagh...pinnnnnnnnnnnnnnnnnnngk...thiiiiiiiiinn-nnnnnnng-haaa...thaaagh... grrreeeeeeeennnnnhaaaa...beeeeeeeeeeeennnnnn." He's totally incoherent.

"WHAT? SPEAK TO ME! HELLO?"

He mumbled again; sounded like pink and green? The pink, I had no clue. The green: Placidyl, extremely heavy duty. I've taken plenty of those.

"How many?" I asked the lump. No response. "Wink. Speak. Something!"

"Threeeeeeeeee...eeeeeeeeeaaaaaach...threeeeeeeeeeee-aaaaaaaaaaaaaach...fugggggggginnnnnnn...gonnnnne."

"Three each? Dude, that's fucking stupid!"

I looked up the pink pills: Heavy-duty psychotropic anti-convulsion meds, mixed with America's second-favorite sleeping pill (after the Lemmon 714). Placidyl is hardcore, and double that sentiment when you mix it with other downer shit. I took one of each, smoked cigarettes, and watched Cal Worthington ride a wild boar who he referred to as his dog, Spot. I took two more of the pills. Mike was catatonic. I watched *The Late Show* and divided the pills up into two piles. Everything got blurry, and I felt myself tipping over in slow motion.

I woke up. I looked at the kitchen clock. Six o'clock. AM or PM? I couldn't tell which; daylight savings really fucks with the head. Mike was still catatonic, breathing weird, slurring, and mumbling a lot of nonsense. The combination of drugs had created lockjaw. He said he snorted coke that someone brought over, thinking it would straighten him out. He was slurring and rambling now. Again, I looked at the kitchen clock. It was 6:30 PM. Wow, eighteen hours out, gone, comatose.

"I gotta go."

"Wait, come with me to Tujunga." He said through a clenched jaw. His right hand snapped up involuntarily. More effects of the drug mix, I guess.

"No way, dude. Fuck that. My mom's gonna freak."

"It's OK, just going to take some of the pills to Tujunga, to that dude, and trade them for some speed or some more coke."

"What? We can't drive there, not in your car." It was a green BMW 320i. It was brand new just a year ago. Now it was a different story.

"Come on, I can't go alone. Do a line, I still have a little coke."

So I did a line, and then we were in the BMW. We were on the 101, heading to the 170 north—all good so far. Then we got pulled over, just as we are making the connection from one freeway to the other. Just two young gentlemen in a late-model Bimmer, back window shot out from a drug deal gone wrong, side-view mirror being held on by a string-thingy. No seats; one of us sat on a milk crate, the other on an old piece of luggage. The cop stood there, shaking his head, completely baffled by it all. He stood looking at the back window and the interior.

I started to explain and Mike stopped me.

"Shut up and I'll handle this." He slurred at me.

"Sir, license and registration. And what the fuck is this?"

Mike quickly reached above the visor and grabbed the paperwork.

"Sir, I've had a hell of a.... Officer, this fucking wetback shot at me when I cut him off."

"Son, watch your filthy fucking mouth when you're

speaking to me."

I was nervous and paranoid, desperately trying not to look fucked up.

"Sorry, Officer. I was out at these horse-riding stables and these cracker ranch hands roughed me up and I got a sliver here and maybe another one over here, and now I think I have lockjaw, sir," he rattled incessantly. He paused. Maybe a little more convincing was required?

"To top it off, these animals, these pieces of shit—sorry, these *animals*—stole my Recaro racing seats right out from under us!" By then he was crying, and I was pretty sure they were real tears; he had worked himself into a frenzy. The breakdown had been imminent, and here it was...and not a second too late. It was amazing. Real tears, and really good, quick lies.

"Where are you going now, son?"

"To Valley Presbyterian Hospital. I'm worried the infection has spread. Oh God, please help me, officer!" He was truly hysterical.

"All right, son. Passenger, what is your name?"

"Mike Martin, sir."

"Do you have a license? Can you drive?"

"No, sir. I'm fifteen."

"OK. You two follow me to St. Joe's Hospital, it's closer then Valley Pres."

I laughed while hunkering down on the luggage. The officer led us to the emergency intake at St. Joe's hospital. They gave Mike a tetanus shot, and the officer issued him a fix-it ticket.

A few weeks later, my parents deemed me incorrigible. I was made a ward of the court and sent to a group home. I never saw Mike again.

PARANOID DRIVE

It had been seven months since I "graduated" from my first rehab/TC (therapeutic community). I was put there when I was sixteen and a half. I was completely out of control, stealing from my mother, my stepfather, and quite a few people in the complex we lived in. I stopped going to school and was hanging out with pimps, whores, junkies, thieves, and pornographers; some of them were even friends of my mother and stepfather.

My mom pulled me out of Hollywood High and made me a ward of the court. When I turned 18, I was no longer a minor and they had no choice but to let me out. I had been slowly spiraling back to the behavior that put me there in the first place, trying to control my intake of cocaine, pills, and alcohol, while committing petty thefts and burglaries. I had all of them convinced that I was OK. *I* was even convinced I was OK. But once again, I was living with my mother, the alcoholic, and her boyfriend, the drug dealer.

My father would pick me up to spend weekends at his house in Newport Beach. First we would drive to his office, deep in the heart of Beverly Hills. He was obviously in cahoots with his bank; there was no doubt he was laundering money through them. He did jewelry deals by appointment only, meeting with "associates"—guys with whom he bought and sold diamonds, watches, antiques, and automobiles— while I was sneaking bumps out of a little vial. I'd pop into the restroom while my father was negotiating his shady deals. It was good, clean blow I stole from my mother's boyfriend. I'd come back into the room and they'd be speaking openly about larceny, murder, and whores, taking my coke paranoia to an even more elevated level. If I wasn't already a seasoned professional, trying to hide this could have been tricky.

There was this one day in 1982 when he finished his business and we left Beverly Hills. We went over Coldwater Canyon and made our way to the 101 South. We were tooling along in his new white 450SL, KNX News Radio playing in the background. My father wore a Brooks Brothers suit, custom made alligator loafers, a diamond-encrusted platinum Rolex President dripping from his wrist, and a 2-carat VVS1 pinky ring. And although he never practiced Judaism or acknowleged Jewish holidays, he rocked an obnoxious diamond-and-gold Star of David necklace.

From what I learned in therapy, it seemed my father wore his self-esteem on his sleeve. The therapist talked about it in our multi-family group. He questioned my father about his constant need to put money and materialism before love and concern for my sister and me. This accusation aggravated my father. At the end of our third and final session, he got out of the folding metal chair, casually pushed it together and hurled through a sliding glass window like a Frisbee. A few parents (including two fathers) let out a high-pitched scream.

One man got up and said, "Hey man, come on. He's only here to help you and your family."

My father growled in return, "Sit down, cocksucker, before you lose an eye."

The man backed up jaw agape, complete terror in his eyes.

Then my father walked up to the counselor, bent down, and looked him in the eye. "Listen, you phony piece of community college waste, I spent seven years in reformatories and prison. I won't even mention the numerous jail stints. Your faggoty motherfucking ideas about me, and how I should raise *my* kids, is fairytale *Waltons*-type shit. You're lucky I didn't throw you through that window." He jerked his thumb at me at me, "This kid is an alcoholic, a drug addict, and a thieving, manipulating, lying little piece of shit. Focus on him and his inability to change all that. We're done here. Send me a bill for the window. And again, be happy it wasn't your wannabe-Freudian motherfucking ass that went through it."

These memories were broken by, "So you all right? You off all that shit? Don't fucking lie to me. You get drunk or high at my house this weekend and I'll beat you down good. That's not a threat, it's a promise." He put up his fist. *"From the Good Hands people."* He was quoting the Allstate slogan, but now it was his slogan.

"Yeah Dad, I'm fine. That place really helped me." I was convinced it had. Nonetheless I was paranoid; I still had that vial of blow in my pocket.

"Yeah, seemed like a decent place, until they tried to blame me. None of that shit was my fault; that's all your problem, kid. Anyway, it's got to come from you. No matter what fucking place you're in. Man up, motherfucker, and take responsibility. Or be doomed to a foul fucking meaningless existence."

Just then an announcement on KNX News: *"...John Belushi, dead at 33 of an apparent overdose...."*

We both looked at each other. I was instantaneously devastated and shocked. What the hell? First time one of my heroes died. Really twisted me up.

"Sad fucking shit, huh Mikey?" Dad was shaking his head.

"Yeah." I was in a daze. I loved the guy. Loved his comedy. I looked up to him. I saw him live. Him and Dan Aykroyd, "The Blues Brothers," opened for Steve Martin at the Universal Amphitheatre. I was thinking about all this when my father reminded me, "Remember when we saw *Animal House*? Theater was packed. We laughed our asses off.... What a loss. Fucking drugs, Mikey. See, once again. Don't go down that road. You'll loose everything, like Belushi. Poor fat, funny bastard lost his fucking life, fat fucking junkie." We made our way past the Highland Avenue exit. "Fucking Hollywood. Even when people get what they want, they get taken out. Insatiable shit-hole in the gut that can't be filled with anything."

"*Yeah, whatever, hypocrite,*" I thought to myself.

We drove past the Cahuenga Boulevard exit. "These hotels, these low-rent, shit-stained apartments and tenements," He pointed left and right of the freeway. "You kick down any of those doors in those rat- and roach-infested destitute dwellings and you'll find a lot of wine drinking, dope shooting, freebasing, cock sucking and ass fucking."

"Yeah." I knew it was all true. Hollywood was rife with all of it, and I couldn't stay away.

He continued, "These scummy pimps would put their own mammies on the stroll, stomp their guts on the curb if the money wasn't correct. It's love/hate with those niggers, because those same fucking pimps spend a lot of money with me, buying watches, jewelry and antiques. I also get a commission off the cars I sell them through Leo at Ferraris West. But outside of all that, they're fucking lowlifes. You can add those Beverly-Hills-sand-nigger-Shah-of-Iran motherfuckers to the list, too. Not just them, these scummy beaner gang bangers and the white fucking trash that pop off the Greyhound bus from Des Moines thinking they are gonna be the next Harrison Ford or Olivia Newton-John. Sadly, they end up selling their little pussies on Sunset or their cocks and assholes on Santa Monica. Fucking gonorrhea fest. Then there's that other breed. The scariest. The fucking *goyim* guy who looks like your common everyday blue-collar Joe, who hunts and kills these poor little wayward cocksuckers. You remember that Freeway Killer? More like the Freeway Faggot, fucking and killing those young boy hitchhikers. I know all this shit. I know LA, Mikey. I know California. Inside and outside, from top to bottom."

He tuned it to a jazz station—Duke Ellington. My dad loved jazz, big band, and show tunes. *Cabaret* and *Funny Girl* were cassettes he played quite frequently. Sometimes singing, *"No one is going to rain on my parade..."* along with Barbara Streisand at the top of his lungs. He did this with the top down, in city traffic. I would slouch down in the seat.

"Dad, every city has its bad areas. Look where you grew up—South Bronx."

"Lemme tell you about the South Bronx. I know my way in and out of there like a Chink knows his way through chow mein. Los Angeles is a whole different deal. Not as segregated, spread out. It's easy to navigate and disappear. Mikey, if you think all cities are the same, you're kidding yourself. Some third-world shitbag robbed my friend Irv Frankel of his Rolex President right in his driveway on Canon Drive. Heart of fucking Beverly Hills, man."

I knew Irv Frankel. He was shady.

"Dad, come on. Irv? The same guy who insured that twenty-carat tennis bracelet for his wife, and it disappeared the next week? That Irv Frankel? The guy who claims he was carjacked for his Bentley and he didn't have a scratch on him, and the Bentley was found torched in Bellflower? The guy who burned down his cut-and-sew operation in the Garment District? You called it Jewish lightning."

"Hey asshole, this was different. This fucking really happened, his neighbor witnessed it. How the fuck did you know all that other shit?"

"I heard you talking about it on the phone, Dad. About Irv, about everyone."

He backhanded me in the head.

"Shut the fuck up and mind your own business, little fucking scumbag drug addict."

I felt sick to my stomach immediately. I touched my head and already felt a lump from the two-carat VVS1 pinky ring. I said nothing. Fear shook me to the core. I'd stopped crying years ago. I felt hate rise up like a volcano. Fighting back was futile; he was a 6-foot-6, ex-Golden Gloves boxer and a state-raised lunatic.

It'd been a while since he hit me. Two years ago he pulled me up out of bed at seven in the morning and punched me in the face about three times. He claimed I had known all about the 502 (drunk driving) arrest my sister got the evening before.

"You deserved a couple good punches to the face to jog your memory about never lying to me again."

I kept track of each punch, each backhand, each verbally abusive word he said. It was like I used it as a conversion chart to keep lying and stealing from him. I'd creep into his room at night while he slept to his steal money, peeling bills off a fat wad. He always walked around with five or ten grand on him. He kept it on the nightstand, next to a loaded .44 (he also kept a shotgun next to the bed). Many times I'd thought about shooting him in the face while he slept; I saw it all go down in my head. I also imagined if he woke up, he would grab one of the firearms and shoot me. That's what made it so good—the adrenaline of stealing money and looking at the guns while he lay there sleeping was second to none. Well, maybe a big hit off the pipe, or even a couple Quaaludes. But that's where the money was going, anyway.

Sometimes when I was really high, I would sneak a peak at my stepmother under the covers. She had an incredible body and she slept in the nude. Once, I was stroking her thigh; she woke up and asked me what the hell I was doing, I told her I was looking for the cat. She told me to get out, and if my dad woke up he'd kill me. The next morning at breakfast was awkward; thank God she didn't say anything to him. I was terrified I'd get a real beating.

He'd turn on a dime. One minute he'd be beating the shit

out of me, 10 minutes later he'd ask me if I wanted to go play miniature golf, go to Wendy's, or go see a matinee.

"Want to go to dinner, Mikey? We'll go out to The Crab Cooker and then we'll hang out by the beach. Still a lot of hot pussy down there, even this time of the year."

I didn't want to go anywhere with that maniac. But I had no choice, so I just agreed. Six months, later I ran away.

#1 SON

James and Johnny Lee were pimps from Kentucky. I met them in the billiards room of the Oakwood Garden Apartments clubhouse. Oakwood. A large complex with buildings lettered A to Z. It sat in the Hollywood Hills, above the Warner Brothers lot, next to the Forest Lawn cemetery. It was the purgatory in-between.

James and Johnny had swagger, hardcore swagger, country cum laude, city-made, gangsters. James was an ex-con, rough-and-tumble, streetwise, rugged-outdoor motherfucker. Johnny was suave, debonair, and a little older. He had straightened hair pulled into a ponytail; a clean, well-groomed, manicured killer. He was patient, quiet, and had dead, still eyes. He was *laying back in the cut*, taking it all in. They both wore impeccably tailored suits, looking to hustle any comers, new or old. I knew better than to play pool for money with anybody in here. Even though the place was relatively quiet, it attracted a criminal element—which was fine by me. I was frequently bored and I was always looking for something to get into. I grew tired of my peers, except for maybe skateboarding or going to see music. But that was growing old, too. I gravitated towards crime, drama, drugs, and alcohol. It was just that way. It gave me life, energy, and a very real sense of power.

The Barry Gibb-Barbara Streisand duet "Guilty" played on the overhead sound system. Lithographs of old

Hollywood stars and boulevard scenes of yesteryears gone by littered the walls. The whole décor had a brown motif. The walls and the carpet, both caramels in paired color.

On the opposite end of the room, an older couple, most likely tourists, played shuffleboard on a 22-foot-table. The woman was singing along with Babs. *"(It ought to be illegal) Make it a crime to be lonely or sad..."* she belted out, jumping and squealing after the clinking of a couple of metal pucks. Her man jumped in front of her. He moved hand up and down, putting his index finger to his lips. He was visibly embarrassed and afraid of what anybody might think. She didn't care. She was in Hollywood, playing shuffleboard with the stars.

I had seen James and Johnny a couple of times around the clubhouse and the pool, gave them the heads up sign, but we never formally met. I was fascinated by the way they strutted through the clubhouse, oblivious or just not giving a fuck about rules, etiquette, etc. I was hitting balls around the table. I saw James in my peripheral. Then he leaned in, and made eye contact with me. "Hey man, you cool?" he asked while polishing down his solid black with mother-of-pearl inlay pool cue. It glimmered from the overhead fluorescent lighting.

"Huh? Yes. Yeah, I'm cool." I was nervous. Taken aback. He grinned hard.

"Nah man, do you know where to get any powder?" He leaned in closer and slowly rubbed his nose with his thumb.

"Oh, you mean cool like *that*. Yeah, I know where." I attempted a shot, but scratched and sunk the cue ball.

My stomach started to knot and turn as it always does with the talk or possibility of cocaine sales and or consumption. I looked around the room. Suddenly I was a little paranoid. I saw a busty blonde girl in the opposite corner of the shuffleboard couple. She was playing pool by herself. She winked at me. I winked back. She leaned over the table to shoot, her tits practically spilling out of her green tube top.

Making eye contact, she ran her tongue over her lips. *I have to meet her. Maybe I can fuck her?* I turned my thoughts to the connection. Eli (Apt. N-304) had that real pearly, uncut, ether-based, bubblegum-smelling rocky shit.

James asked me for a sample. Then he took and made a double bank shot.

"He doesn't do samples." I said, catching the blonde looking at me again.

"Oh, we'll pay," he smiled. "Just keep your cracka fingers out the bindle. We'll take care of you."

"Oh I would never…" I started to say while chalking my cue.

"Shut the fuck up, everybody steps on it. Everybody." He went in for another shot. He had me there. I always fucked with the package. I just couldn't help it. "What does he charge for an eight track?" He asked, his eyes slowly moving back and forth, scanning the room.

"That's what you want as a sample? $350." I smiled at the blonde; she was probably a Hollywood Tropicana girl. I had a mental image of her oiled up in the ring, slipping and sliding those big tits on me, then asking me back to her dressing room. She smiled back.

James snapped his fingers.

"Hello? Pay attention, man. The action's right here, motherfucker. So if we give you 400 and break you off a little piece, will that insure that you won't fuck with it?" He broke out a gold cigarette case and popped it open, offered me a Sherman. I took it. I looked at it. No way he laced this thing. I didn't want to get dusted. Not then, anyway.

"Come on man, don't trip, that shit ain't dipped."

"Yeah, yeah man." I was nervous, "I don't want to fuck up a good thing." *I don't want to get pistol-whipped. Or shot.*

He grabbed my shoulder, looked me deep in the eyes and said, "No, you don't." He continued, "How's this work, we just give you the paper and let you walk away?"

"No man, I'll call him from that payphone. He'll meet

me in the TV room, all straight up."

"Well, good. Call that motherfucker then." He chalked his cue, took the shoot, and sank the eight.

"I got to see the cash." He eyeballed me hard. First time drug deals are intimate, trust-fueled. You got to play it direct and fearlessly, or you get a real street-style beating, get robbed or killed. I learned this from my stepfather and my own experiences from selling pot and pills, and now I was learning it with coke. James broke out a fat wad, all hundreds, peeled four, and threw it on the green felt of the pool table. I looked around, and then scooped it up quickly.

"I'm going to be clockin' your trick ass. First, go call. Then go in there with those old motherfuckers and sit up there and look at Jerry Dunphy or Tritia Toyota or whoever the hell them old niggas look at, and you stay put till he come through. We watching." He glanced over at his brother. Johnny looked straight ahead. But he heard it all, and nodded his head slowly.

"OK." I was a little scared. *But an easy one-fifty,* I mused nervously. I made the call. Put in the order. I strutted into the TV room, feeling like Lee fucking Iacocca.

Oakwood is a retirement spot; it also housed actors for pilot season. The residents also included some trust funders, plenty of singles, and even a couple of families. Now sprinkle in some R&B singers, burned-out rock 'n' rollers, B-actors and actresses, and call girls. It was a hotbed of alcoholism, sex, drug addiction, and pharmaceutical self-hate. I loved it there. I was a heartless little beast. What did I know? I was just young, dumb, and full of cum, and not afraid to splash it around. The old divorcees and retirees loved to fuck and suck cock. They were so desperate to retain anything that resembled youth. I fucked all kinds of women, young and old. I met them at the jacuzzi, the pool, the clubhouse, or right there in the billiards room. I had no skills, just bullshit fantasies, a gift of gab—salesman-type shit—and a cherubic way of sweeping people off their feet.

My real dreams were crushed by self-sabotage, physical abuse, alcoholism, drug addiction, and negative reinforcement from each and every family member around me. I had just moved up to Oakwood. I stayed there with my alcoholic mother and felonious pill dealing, compulsive gambling, stepfather.

I lived life day to day. My life was all about getting high, drinking, stealing, fucking, eating, manipulating, and lying my way through all of it. I was also trying to show up to Hollywood High School. I was getting progressively worse. It was all spiraling quickly and it wasn't going to stop; my grades and my behavior...just all of it going to shit.

I waited in the back of TV lounge. Three levels of brown leather couches in a darkened wood paneled room. A couple of residents were watching the 11 o'clock news. At the commercial breaks they were speaking about the Iran hostage crisis, and the assassination of John Lennon. My mother was devastated. I didn't really care; I didn't have it in me to care. Death meant nothing to me, it just didn't equate. I didn't think about it; I wasn't that deep. I spent most waking hours thinking of myself. People really didn't matter, unless I could get something from them.

Then Eli walked in. He's wearing tight cut-off Levi 501s and a Mickey Mouse T-shirt and flip-flops. He would pass for James Caan—even had the dirty blonde Jew-fro—if he didn't speak, but then the Israeli accent kills the resemblance.

"Michael." Sounded like he said *Vikal*.

"Hey." I'm trying to hide my anticipation, the excitement I get from brokering any drug deal, large or small, that false sense of importance. I felt needed. One man turned his head and shushed Eli. Eli shushed him back, then sat down next to me. He shook his head and grinned, looking down at the other residents. He put a plain envelope between us. My price was 250; I palmed him the bills and told him I'd collect the change later. He asked about my Mom, Danny, and school. I lied and answered, "Fine."

I heard "*Shh!*" again. Eli grinned and looked down, then yelled, "*Shh* you, Morty! This is all bullshit you're watching. Fucking lying assholes! Bullshit news. Michael, I gotta go."

I looked at the screen. The anchorman was someone I'd see at The Smokehouse restaurant, always drunk as fuck and tooling around in his Rolls.

Eli walked out. I walked out as well. Morty, an old nebbish Jew, grabbed my wrist as I passed. He was sporting a straw hat, Hawaiian shirt, OP shorts, and sandals. He was a Hollywood extra—a day player, literally and figuratively. He had a desperate, sad, lonely look in his eyes.

"Michael, you're a good kid. You've got a lot going for yourself. Stay away from these *gonnifs* and *schvartzes*. You want to come to my apartment, listen to some rock records and smoke grass?" He says this in all earnestness. Morty had offered me a blowjob once. When I refused, he offered to pay me one hundred dollars. I let him suck my dick as I flipped through *Oui* magazine. I still couldn't cum. He gave me the hundred anyway. That was the beginning and the end of my gay prostitute career.

"Morty, I don't got shit going on. And I ain't really that good. But thanks all the same." I walked away.

James Lee was standing outside the lounge. He pointed to the men's room authoritatively, and I followed him in. I passed him the package. He motioned me to be the lookout and went in the stall. I heard him opening the package, then sniffing. He came out, eyes wide, gave me the thumbs up and pointed to the door. We walked back to the billiards area. Johnny was in the same spot he was standing in before, chalking a pool cue. James gave him the all-good sign. Johnny didn't flinch, just nodded his head slowly.

"Yeah, we been out here from Louisville for a hot minute. We need a driver to take the girls to their dates and to the clubs an' whatnot," James said. He pulled a small black case from under the pool table, opened it, pulled out a silk hanky, and methodically cleaned the cue and unscrewed it.

"Shit, I'll do it," I said, having no idea what it even entailed, but volunteering anyway.

Johnny looked me in the eye, then turned back to the table. Shook his his head and grinned. He finally spoke, in a low dark tone: "Nah, man. You're too young. We need someone with skills. Shit gets complicated sometimes." He commenced to run the table on another brother, beating him. Soon the dude was paying Johnny, looked like a couple of hundred dollars. They shook hands and the other guy walked away. "That was Ronnie. He a record producer, he got Hollywood Sound. He can unload a gang a blow."

James said, "You keep that clean, untouched powder coming and we can make a grip, for real."

"Yeah? Well let me know." I started to walk away. I was thinking about that blonde. I didn't see her. *Where did she go? Maybe outside?*

"Yo, where you going?" James Lee asked. "I still owe you a little something something." *Maybe she's out by the pool. Does she live here? Fuck.*

"I was gonna see if there's any girls out by the jacuzzi. See what's going on out there."

"Shit, girls? Man, we got all kinds of pussy up at our crib." I thought of Cal Worthington and rows of women instead of cars. I looked at James, then at Johnny. "Yo bro, take him on up there," he said moving his eyes to the heavens.

I followed James through the glass double doors leading out of the back of the clubhouse. We walked by the pool. It was pretty quiet, just a couple of late-night swimmers and some people talking. It was a typical California evening at the Oakwood Gardens. The twinkling lights of Los Angeles lit a beautiful backdrop of what seemed like somewhere else.

"Just remember, we living in G, unit G-300. G for fucking gangster," he said with a chuckle.

"Ha, yeah," I laughed nervously. I didn't know what the

fuck I was stepping into.

We approached, and I heard Kurtis Blow's "The Breaks" coming through the door. He unlocked it and we went in. It smelled sweet, like coconut oil.

"Yo, Katara! Rose! Snow! Hey ya'll, we got a visitor." We moved quickly into the room, and he shut and locked the door. I stepped into the living room/dining room area. Three beautiful teen or twenty-something girls wearing dolphin shorts and bathing suits sat on a black leather couch around a black lacquer-and-glass coffee table. They looked at me, grinning.

"Hey what's up?' I waved. I was nervous as fuck, overwhelmed by it all. Katara, a tan, curvy brunette with crystal blue eyes, popped off the couch and came up to me. She looked me up and down.

"Who's this?" she said in a Southern drawl, while poking and grabbing my chest.

"Fuck, I dunno. I never even axed yo' name, huh?" James said as he pulled a black Deering coke grinder out of a drawer. My stomach started turning in anticipation of that first line.

"Trip on that shit: Muthafucka gets me an eighth of the clean shit, I don't know his name."

"It's Mike," I said nervously, feeling sized up and judged.

"Mike, these girls probably gonna try to rustle some beef, so be ready," he said as he ground down the coke.

"Huh?"

I couldn't take my eyes off Katara until Rose came up. She was a pixie redhead with a gymnast's body, light freckles, and green eyes. "You a Jew or Eyetalian?" she asked in a trashy Southern accent. "Where you from? Look at this curly Jew-fro, y'all."

Then Snow walked up—a bustier, lustier version of Debbie Harry. An ivory white girl with big brown doe eyes and platinum hair, tits practically falling out of her bathing suit top. She grabbed my cock and said, "I bet this little nigga can fuck all day. How old are you?"

"Sixteen." I croaked, taken aback. It was confusing, exciting, and a little daunting.

"Mmm," she said. "I want some."

"Rustling beef," James Lee repeated, shaking his head as he rotated the top of the grinder. I love the sound of coke being ground down in a Deering.

"Where you stay at?" Rose asked while looking me over and giving Katara the high sign.

"Over in E building. God damn, you three are fucking foxy," I said involuntarily. The three of them grabbed each other's tits and asses, laughing.

"We know," Rose and Snow said in unison.

James put a couple of big lines on a black plate and said, "Here man." He handed me a fresh rolled-up hundred-dollar bill. I took the bill and the plate and hit it hard. I immediately felt it. It dripped down my throat and it was so clean. The euphoria was fantastic—coke that gives me a hard-on, makes my balls tingle. I went to pass it.

"Nah, hit the other side too, man." He pointed at the plate. The girls were watching, and they couldn't wait for their turn. They looked pre-orgasmic, lips full, watery eyes filled with lust, nipples hard. I *got them this coke. I'm the shit. I'm the guy. I'm needed.* I hit it, and again, the sensation was fantastic. That sense of pure Peruvian goodness that only clean, ether-based coke brings. I handed the plate to Katara and sat down on the couch. "Tell Me Something Good" was coming out of the stereo.

I put my head back and closed my eyes. I felt a hand on each knee traveling up my thighs. Rose and Katara were kneeling in front of me, dancing, kissing, and touching each other. I didn't remember ever being that turned on, that overwhelmed with lust. They both took off their tops, kissing each other. James and Snow laughed, and on their way out the door:

"Have fun, y'all."

I heard Snow's voice fade as I was taking off my shirt. They were both taking off their shorts. Katara had beautiful tan lines, smooth, taut, beautiful skin. Completely shaved. Rose was lightly freckled with strawberry nipples, very light pubic hair and a sexy pink pussy. I stood up and almost tripped taking my jeans off. My dick was so hard it hurt.

Rose giggled, "Have you done this before, are you still a virgin?"

"Yes, I've done it, but not with two girls."

She laughed and mimicked me: "*But not with two girls,* ha ha." They were both kissing and biting my skin, my nipples, and my neck.

Katara grabbed my face, looked me in the eye and said, "Kiss me, you sexy little motherfucker." I felt my dick flinch. I kissed her, tasted sweet. Wine sweet. Southern sweet. She was moaning and grabbed my hand and guided it to her pussy. It was so wet. She put two of my fingers in. She grabbed my hand and sucked the wetness off her fingers. Then Rose was on her knees, and had my dick in her mouth. Soft, slow, and then fast, wet. The three of us fucked and sucked for what seemed like hours. Blowing more lines, drinking whiskey, and just laughing and sexing our young asses off.

We all lay on the couch, feet up on the coffee table.

"Where's James and Snow?" I asked.

"James took her to her date," Rose said, passing me a joint. She continued, "Some old rich Texas guy, lives in West Bel Air. They trying to get him to invest in real estate in Louisville. Told him they need $100,000 cash."

I just listened. Suddenly I was scared; I was getting too familiar with what was going on here. I told them I should go. I got up.

Katara grabbed my cock. "No, no, sexy boy. Please stay."

"I'll be back. I have to make an appearance at home, or my mom will freak." I started putting on my clothes. Just then the door opened. James and Snow entered laughing and talking. Snow had bags from Fatburger. James had a beige American Express overnight bag. They both looked happy.

"What's going down, K and Rose? Y'all get what you needed?" he asked, high-fiving Snow and winking.

"Mmhmm. You were right, Snow. This youngin' can fuck all night," Katara said as Rose nodded her head. I felt dirty and humiliated, my intimacies being bandied about.

"Look, I need to jet. I got to be home before my mom wakes up."

"Aw, that's cool. Have a burger, and call your boy. We need a couple of Z's, I mean like a quarter key." He tried to hand me a burger.

"No, I'm not really hungry. What time is it? Wait, a quarter kilo? How many ounces is that? I can't call him now." I was getting nervous, and excited all at once.

"Damn, take a chill pill. It's 3:30 in the mornin', mutha-fucka. That's nine ounces, son. That nigga ain't 24/7?" James continued, "Must be a honky!"

They all laughed. I was already putting numbers together in my head; I could probably make a thousand dollars on this kind of a deal.

James started dumping the contents of the small travel bag. Stacks and stacks of rubber-banded bills tumbled onto the dining room table. He started stacking it, then stopped, walked over and bolted and chained the door.

"We got to count this, make sure it's correct. That old motherfucker...well, he a little fickle. Come on Rose."

I started to move towards the table.

"Nah man, not you. We don't know how you be around a lot of paper," he said, putting his hand up. "What time that nigga open shop? That's your job." He and Rose were already counting bills.

"I could call at 8 AM." I felt insulted, not getting to count the money. Now I didn't want to leave, but I knew I

had to. "Alright then, I'll come back at around at 8 or 9."
I started putting on my shoes. Vans leather slip-ons, grey
and blue. My school colors. I barely ever made it to school.
When I did, I was 'luded out, drunk, or just not able to be
present. The only thing that made sense was creative writing
or making pipes in metal shop.

"Aw c'mon," Rose said. James smacked her on the head
with a quick backhand. "Owww, dammit." Her eyes quickly
started watering.

"Bitch, you had your fun, stop hounding that motherfucker! Get in there and wash yo' pussy, it stank! Damn
trifling ho."

I quickly put on my shirt, totally uncomfortable with
what I just witnessed. "OK, later man. I'll come by tomor-
row." I got out of there.

I walked back home, to E-302. I laid in bed and thought
about it all, I was so excited I couldn't sleep. *Should I just
stay up?* I knew where my mom kept Desoxyn—pharmaceutical methamphetamine; I crept into her room while
they slept, and I found it. She was an RN, she had a plethora of pills. I would find the pills and then research them in
her *Physician's Desk Reference*, an encyclopedia of pictures
and information about all the latest pharmaceutical medications. I wanted to stay up. I did not want to miss out on the
chance of that coke deal. I lay in bed and read *Surfer, High
Times*, and *Hustler* magazines. The minutes went by like
hours. The Desoxyn made my scalp tingly and my mouth
was bone-dry. I got up to get some water. It was 6 AM.

"Whaddya' say there kid?" my stepfather's phlegmy
Bronx accented voice came up from behind me. I jumped.

"Whoa, shit! Fuck, Dan!" I was suddenly paranoid.

"What's the matter kid, can't sleep? You want something?" He ambled out to the kitchen.

"No. Yes. What do you got?" He put on the kettle, took
a pastry box off the top of the fridge and methodically cut
off a piece of the cheese Danish. Then he sat down and lit a

Merit cigarette. He smoked and ate the Danish simultaneously. Danny, or Dr. Dan, Dr. Quaalude, Dr. Dildo...those were his self-made monikers. Danny was an old-school Bronx Jew, came up hard. Daniel Samuel Faigenbaum. Between bites, he broke it down.

"Well, I got 'ludes, Doriden, Placidyl, reds, rainbows, Valium." He loved to tout his wares. He was truly a street doctor. A parade of people came in and out of the apartment. Car salesmen, studio laborers, attorneys, a mattress salesmen, housewives, and just plain street junkies, they came day after day. They were all hurting. He made them feel better. Danny took care of them for better or worse. It was what it was.

"Uh, give me one of each." I laughed. I wanted to eat something but I knew I couldn't.

"Asshole, you get one—one pill." He got up and started walking to his bedroom.

"OK let me try the Placidyl, the green one." I already knew what 'ludes did, I had already stolen quite a few as well. I wanted something new. I tried to eat a piece of Danish. I gagged. It wasn't going to happen. I drank some water instead.

The apartment was a two-bedroom, had old furniture, a tan threadbare shag rug, torn up in the corners. There were always pills, coke or money under a corner of the carpet. Danny had two VHS players hooked up to a nineteen-inch Sony Trinitron console television. He would make bootleg copies all day long, usually first-run Hollywood movies, or the newest porno films. Danny acquired these from insiders in both industries. He would trade pills, coke or pot for them (for pennies on the dollar) and sell them for a premium. He had so many hustles going on at once, it was hard to keep up. He came out with the pill. He made his way back to the Danish, and handed me the pill on the way.

"What are you doing today, kid?" he asked, spitting crumbs my way.

"Oh you know, just hanging out." That was an out-and-out lie. He made his way over to the VCRs. He hit play on one and record on another while talking about the difference between the Doriden and the Quaaludes.

Soon an image appeared on the screen. Then a couple of minutes after that, Vanessa Del Rio was getting butt-fucked by Ron Jeremy. Danny was telling another story about growing up in the Bronx. He was totally oblivious to the sights and sounds coming out of the color console, where Vanessa was moaning and groaning, getting hard anal. All the while Danny was pontificating about the difference between *blacks* and *niggers*. I'd heard it before; he tended to repeat himself every three months or so.

"So what, is there two types of Jews too?" I said, taking it all in.

"Yeah, there are the broken-down, schmucky, *schnorrer* Jews who have no money and who hate themselves," he said, while spitting pieces of coffee soaked Danish and smoking a cigarette and looking at the NFL point spreads in the sports section of the *LA Times*.

"OK, and the other kind of Jew?" I asked, watching Ron finish off in Vanessa's ass.

He was still looking at the paper and the morning line. "This fucking Sonny Reizner at Castaways.... Jesus kid, he knows his shit." He was referring to the guy who ran the sports book in Vegas, but I really wanted to know the other types of Jew.

"Dan, please. The other type of Jew! What is that Jew about?" A new scene was starting on TV. Apparently Ms. Del Rio was a sex therapist with a TV-style audience in this porno tape. She was fucking and sucking everyone in the audience. It looked pretty good.

"Schmuck! The ones with money! The ones that aren't broken-down suitcases! The ones that are tough, that can fight and survive any fucking thing!" Now he was really spitting and clearly pissed. "Don't you have to go to fucking school?" He growled, taking a pen and writing some list of things to do, while rifling through a phonebook/organizer.

"No it's Saturday. Damn. Take it easy, man. Fuck."

I went in my room. It was 7:45 AM. *I'll get dressed and go to the clubhouse. Call Eli, and then go see James Lee. Or should I see James Lee first? Well sure, I must get the money first.* I threw on some clothes. "OK, later Dan." He was still flipping through his phonebook. He waved me off without looking up.

I was starting to feel the fatigue. The Desoxyn was wearing off, wearing thin. I needed more of something in the stimulant family. I walked downstairs. Cars pulled out of the parking structures, the day was just starting. People were on their way to jobs, auditions, and creative gigs, all going somewhere. Fuck them. I'm glad I didn't have to be a part of that shit. I walked back to G building. It was dead quiet in G-304. I knocked.

"Yeah, who dat?" The voice was quick, and perplexed. I was ready to turn and walk, I felt paranoid. Then I heard the deadbolt slowly turn, and the door opened. Johnny stood there in a black silk robe over black pajamas. The robe was monogrammed in red with *JL* above the right chest pocket.

We stood looking at each other for a minute. Then Rose stepped out in a little pink nightie. "Well come in, motherfucker."

This guy scared me. He wasn't as jovial and chill as James. I walk in. He motioned me to sit at the small dining room table. Rose brought him a cup of coffee. He slapped her hard in the ass. "Bitch, go put your robe on. Just 'cuz this motherfucker had his dick in you, that don't mean you strut around like you his bitch. Get that shit straight, ho."

She quickly ran in the other room.

"So that powder good, you gonna get us a discount on that quarter key?" He said while stirring some sugar into black coffee. Rose came back out in a pink robe. She went into the kitchen. Just as I was going to answer, Johnny cut in. "Rose, scramble him some eggs." He pointed at me, and made an eating motion.

"Yeah, that would be great. Listen man, I don't know how much he charges for that." I felt nervous, amateurish and out of place. Rose put a cup of coffee down in front of me.

"Man, I know you don't. Motherfucker, you probably ain't slung more than an ounce or two. Your young ass."

Rose put a plate of eggs and toast in front of me. She smiled, "You want cream and sugar? Johnny generally drinks it black, don't you J?"

He waved her off. "Bitch, you dismissed. Go wake up them other hos. Y'all finta be ready for The Seventh Veil later, Tricky Rick coming by to pick y'all up. Do not keep that nigga waiting."

She walked away.

"Rose, DO NOT." He raised his voice. "Damn, acknowledge me, bitch."

"OK, Johnny, OK. We will not keep Tricky waiting, my word."

He was shaking his head. "These bitches all good, but you can't let them slack for a minute."

"Yeah, I don't know." I sat there dumbfounded. I had seen my father (and my stepfather) call women names, yell and even smack them around once or twice. This was a totally different situation.

"No you don't. You better off, too. This is no sucker game. I was learnt all this by my uncle." He sat and stared straight ahead as he spoke. Trance-like. "These bitches ain't nothing, and they'll work you and get you to pay for the pussy any way they can. Fuck all that. These bitches pay they own way, get all the dick and dope they want. Ho's line my pockets and pay for all this bullshit." He waved his hand in the air. "I go out and do my own hustles, bigger-dollar shit. Because bitches come and go."

I just sat there. I felt tension and fear in my sleep-deprived body.

"Hey man, I'm fading. You got any of that left from last night?" I asked.

"Yeah man, first holla' at ya' boy. We need some weight." He got up, walked to the kitchen area and grabbed the phone.

"Hey, um, it might be better for me to go talk to him in person. I feel freaked out asking him for that kind of deal over the phone. You know what I mean?"

He came and sat down across from me. I sat and took a forkful of eggs. They were super salty, but good nonetheless. I was glad that I could eat.

"Yo, look at me. This ain't no mufuckin' eight track we talking, you feel me? You can go talk and lounge and listen to music, shit whatever the fuck you want, then come on back and gimme the right price. But I expect this shit go down quick once I fund it, kid. Ya got it? I ain't sitting round here like a fiend waiting on a half gram, staring at the walls and shit. No, uh-uh, that ain't me. I'm controlling this shit, you a runner. Period. We clear?"

I looked him right in the eyes. Dark eyes, I couldn't even see the pupils. I knew if I fucked with this guy in any way, shape or form, he'd probably beat me within an inch of my life. You can read that in a man's eyes. My father had the same glance, same look. I took some heavy ass-whippings from him.

"Yes." There was nothing else to say.

"Well let's do the damn thing. It's 9:45. That motherfuck-er in the complex?" He said sitting back and clasping his hands. He knew this already. He was testing me for bullshit.

"Yes." I said, as I ate the last bit of toast and eggs.

"He sure is. I expect you back within 45 minutes. Go. Don't waste time." I got up and grabbed my empty plate and cup to bring to the sink. "Yo, leave that shit, this ain't your momma's house. Them ho's cook and clean up in this piece."

That made me chuckle, and he grinned. I unchained and

unbolted the door. He was already behind me. I closed the door and heard it bolt and the chain replaced.

I was fading. Shit. I wanted to ask for a line. I knew that might piss him off since I hadn't done the deal or even made contact yet. I walked past the pool. A couple of people were already lying out. I saw the busty blonde from the billiards room. She looked so fucking foxy. *God, I want to fuck this girl, please let that happen.* Her skin was glistening with oil, and she was wearing a pink one-piece bathing suit, her blonde hair a beacon of light. I couldn't stop looking, and tripped over a Malibu light. I fell into some shrubbery. She looked at me and smiled. She waved me over. I felt embarrassed, but walked over nonetheless.

Then I heard, "Hi Mike." I looked around. "Over here, son." Over at the other side of the pool was Morty. He was waving his big straw hat. I was pissed. *Fuck that guy, always in my business. Shit.*

"Yeah, yeah, hi," I said, uninterested. The girl had turned over on her stomach and was watching all this go down. *Goddamn it Morty. You're a fucking bummer,* I whispered to myself.

"Hi, I'm Mike." I said awkwardly as I approached her. I felt a little confidence from my activities the night before. Not a total loser.

"Hi. I'm Bambi. Hey is that your dad over there?" she asked as she scratched her right thigh. She turned onto her side, toward me. Her tits were were spilling out of the top of her bathing suit.

"No, just some old dude always trying to talk to me."

"Yeah I get that too," she said with a chuckle. She was looking me in the eyes and still rubbing the oil on her inner thighs. I guessed her to be late teens or early twenties. We looked at each other for a minute. Nothing awkward, just silence. Taking each other in. "What were you doing hanging out with those pimps the other night?"

"Oh, those guys are pimps?" I asked sheepishly. She

grinned at me.

"Who the hell do you think they were?" She retorted.

"I thought they were insurance agents." We both laughed. She turned and lay on her back, opening and closing her legs slowly. Her tits were spilling out of the side of her bikini, and I felt myself starting to get erect. *I have to get to Eli's,* I thought. "Those guys just needed me to do something, it's kind of a long story." I said, standing up.

"Where you going?" She rose out of the lounge. "Come swimming with me." She said turning her back to me. The bikini had crept between her ass and her cheeks were showing. Her body was perfect.

"Listen, I just got to go do something. I'll be back in a little while."

"For the insurance agents?" She laughed.

"Yeah. Can I see you later?" She stopped and turned around. "Sure. If I'm not here by the pool, come to my apartment. I live in B-106. B, as in boy."

"OK. I will." I watched her turn and walk away, her tight bubble butt glistening and jiggling ever so slightly in the California sun.

With a spring in my step, I walked over to Eli's apartment. From behind the door I could hear Middle Eastern music and what sounded like arguing in Hebrew. I knocked on the door. Suddenly it was silent. Then yelling, then a phone slammed on its base. "Yes please, who is there?" A female voice asked. It was Ariella.

"Vikal," I said in a mock-Yiddish voice. The door unbolted, unchained and opened. Ariella. Oh God, Ariella, Eli's girlfriend. She stood there, flawless, with her light olive skin. She was on her way out to the pool, wearing a black bikini. She was tall, had green eyes, and dark black hair. An Israeli Brigitte Bardot. An Israeli Sophia Loren. I had beat off to the image of this woman at least ten times. Busty and lusty is an understatement. When I first saw her, I wanted to go live on a kibbutz, but Danny talked me out of it. She was a model for the Gottex bathing suit company.

"OK, hi Michael. I'm leaving. Eli is in shower. He will be out soon. Please help yourself to drink, eat whatever, I go now." She walked out.

I watched her smooth ass cheeks dance back and forth in the tiny bikini bottoms. She turned and smiled. I was caught in the act of ass-gazing, as usual.

"Bye bye."

Even her broken English made me horny.

I went in and sat on the couch. Framed posters of Israel were scattered on the walls. There was cushy beige couch sectional, a La-Z-Boy chair, and big entertainment center, with a Sony Trinitron, a top-of-the-line Marantz stereo system, and a TEAC reel-to-reel tape player. It was moving and quietly playing the music I heard earlier. I looked around quickly while I heard the shower going.

What can I take that won't be noticed? I saw a small leather bag on the top shelf of the entertainment center. I jumped off the couch and high-stepped over to it on the balls of my feet. I grabbed it, and unzipped the bag. There was a large bag of chunky coke, and many small bags already weighed out. My guess was grams and eighths; I knew he didn't sell anything less then a gram. I thought it best to take from the bigger bag. I heard the shower go off. Then singing, the same song I'd heard earlier. *Oh shit,* I whispered involuntarily. I quickly opened the bag and grabbed a half-dollar sized rock. I placed it on top of the reel to reel closed the bag put it back. I had it in my hand and no clue where to put it. *Fuck, fuck, fuck...!*

I looked on the table, at a big yellow legal pad. The front page had a numbered list of things written in Hebrew. I quickly ripped a page from the middle, fashioned a bindle, and threw the coke in. I put it in my pocket and casually walked to the fridge.

"Hello?" Eli called from the bathroom. I opened the fridge and grabbed a Fresca.

"Hey man, it's Mike." I went and sat at the dining room table, far from the leather bag and its contents.

"Ah, Vikal. Ariella let you in? Is she here?"

"I think she went down to the pool." I heard a blow dryer go on and I was really starting to fade. I wanted to go hit some of this blow that was in my pocket. I moved toward the bathroom.

"ELI," I yelled over the blow dryer.

"WHAT?" He turned off the blow dryer and ran out of the bathroom. He was visibly shaken.

"Can I use the bathroom?"

"What the fuck? Yes, yes. You don't have to ask. Go use it in the spare bedroom. Don't wake Effie. He was in the war, he might kill you." He laughed.

"I know, you told me before." He was serious.

Effie was in some combat situation, the Three-Day War or some shit. He saw some blood and guts. As a result of that, he suffered from PTSD and often woke up in violent fits. Eli used him for heavy work—unpaid credit lines, dealers who fucked with packages, etc.

I slowly opened the door. The snoring was so loud I shuddered. I crept past him. The room was a mess. There were clothes and shoes strewn about, half-eaten food items on plates, empty wine bottles, papers and documents. On the walls, *Playboy*, *Oui*, and *Hustler* magazine centerfolds were haphazardly slapped up.

I was watching my every step for fear of rattling or breaking something and waking this maniac. Between snoring, he snapped up and screamed something in Hebrew. I jumped. Then he lay down and started snoring again. I made it to the bathroom and shut the door. I open the little bindle quickly. I took a little piece off the rock, put it on top of the toilet tank. I crushed it with my house key and made it snortable. I rolled up a bill very quickly and snorted up both lines. WOW! It hit my septum. I quickly put the coke away. I felt brand new. *It's all going to be OK.* I got excited about the deal, the blonde by the pool, the whores....

Suddenly all of it was broken by screaming and pounding on the door. "Who the fuck is in there, man? I keel you! MOTH-A-FUCKA!" *Bam, bam, bam!*

I jumped and fell backwards through the shower curtain. Then more pounding on the door, and what sounded like a kick. Then I hear Eli start yelling in Hebrew, Effie yelling back. Then in English I hear: "Seet the fuck down Effie! Vikal, come out. It's OK."

I slowly rose out of the tub, clenching a bottle of Herbal Essence shampoo. My heart was racing. I checked my pocket for the Placidyl; I quickly ate it. I cleaned the coke residue off the toilet. I came out. Effie was sitting on the bed.

"You OK?" Eli asked. "I told you not to wake him."

"Yeah man, fuck. I didn't wake him. Goddammit." My heart was pounding in my chest. I stood near the door. We looked back and forth at each other. "Can we go out on the balcony and talk?"

"I told you not to wake him, Michael." He was grinning.

"Eli, you're kidding, right? I fucking tiptoed through the room." We walked out to the living room. "Maybe he's doing too much coke."

He looked pensive.

"What? That guy shouldn't do *any* coke! None!"

"Vikal, don't judge; that's my brother."

"OK, whatever. I'm just saying, he was in the war and, well.... Listen, these guys want more."

He walked toward the entertainment center and picked up the bag. My heart was pounding. *Will he notice that chunk of coke that's gone? I'm sure he will. He accounts for every gram. Maybe he'll suspect Effie?*

"Why didn't you say so?"

"Yes. But they want a quarter key." He put the bag back.

"Oh, OK. They have the money?" He went toward the table and looked down at his list.

"Oh yeah, they got it. Do you want to meet them?"

He was shaking his head, "No, no, I don't want to meet anyone. I want you to bring me $11,000, your cost."

"OK, Eli. Where should we do it?"

He looked towards Effie's room.

"Not here. The TV room is fine, in and out. I'll be there in 20 minutes. No bullshit, make sure all the money is there...or you can deal with my brother." He laughed and pointed to Effie's room.

"Will it be good as last night?" I wasn't amused by the Effie comment.

"It will be the same product as last night. Don't try to get rich on this. Just add your commission and I'll reimburse later. Maybe you add $100 per once. If you try to get more then that, they'll know you're trying to fuck them. You will ruin a future opportunity."

I thought about that for a minute; I always ruined future opportunities. I walked toward the door. I heard Effie scream in the other room, and what sounded like a door being kicked or punched. It sent a shiver through me.

Eli picked up the newspaper and started reading. I imagined him as an orderly in a nuthouse, desensitized to the insanity around him.

"Vikal?" He said without raising his head from the paper.

"Yes?" I turned and looked back, my hand on the doorknob.

"Twenty minutes."

"Yes, got it." I walked out. I started running, elated, excited, and on my way to the biggest deal I'd ever made. I ran down the stairs towards G building, my head spinning with visions of coke, whores, and money.

I approached the clubhouse and leasing office, then I heard loud exhaust rumbling and Supertramp's music just above that. It was *Breakfast in America*. I knew it was Steve Anders. He always drove through the complex blasting tunes in his new blue Trans Am. Texas plates. T-tops off and windows down. He always wore a cowboy hat and Vuarnet sunglasses. He had been warned by security about his driving, but he told him to fuck off. His dad was a VIP resident at Oakwood. He managed a white-bread family band that was topping the charts, and leased quite a few apartments for them and their entourage.

He yelled to me: "Hey jerkoff, where ya running to?" He sounded as black and country as my newfound friends. He parked the car in the red and jumped out, never opening the door. I backed up as he approached. He knew karate and enjoyed showing me moves, occasionally practicing it on me. Even though it wasn't full-contact, it felt awkward and uncomfortable, like dancing at an after-school event.

"Yeah, hey man." I was still walking.

"Hey, I'm talking to you, slick."

I stopped and turned around. He looked me in the eyes.

"Man. You look fuccckkked up! What are you on, partner?"

"I'm right in the middle of something man, I gotta jet." He came up and grabbed my arm.

"Slow down, hero. You seen Heidi? Where is that bitch?" Heidi was Steve's on-again, off-again girlfriend. He was obsessed with her. She'd come to LA from Wichita Falls to model. She was young, blonde, and terribly naïve, but a total fucking fox.

"No, I haven't seen her. I gotta go, man."

"I seen you walking around with them pimp niggers. They're bad news, my dad buys coke off of them."

"Just friends, man." I kept walking.

"Yeah, bullshit. Them motherfuckers ain't no good. If you see Heidi, tell her to come to my apartment."

"I will, man, I will."

He turned and walked back to the car, cranked Supertramp's "Logical Song" and burned rubber up the road.

I made it back to Johnny's. I knocked on the door. I heard whispering behind the door. Then the door unlatched. Johnny stood there in a red silk shirt and designer jeans.

"Come in, man." I entered the room. I looked over at the couch. Katara and Heidi were sitting there. Coke was lined up on a black plate on the coffee table. I looked at Heidi.

"Steve is looking for you. I just saw him." She waved her hand. I turned back to Johnny.

"Fuck that cracker hillbilly," he said. "She in our car now. More importantly, how much that motherfucker gonna hit me on the quarter key?" I got nervous. I added one hundred an ounce in my head. Easy enough, nine ounces equals nine hundred, round it up. "12,000—twelve thousand dollars."

I heard Rose mimic me in the other room and laugh.

"Nigga, just say 12K or 12G. You ain't gotta get all specific up in this motherfucker. You sound like rookie vice and shit."

He looked over at Katara and winked. "That's a good price though. Glad you ain't greedy. I hate a greedy motherfucka. I mean especially after I treat him to all my shit. When's it happening?" He looked back in the living room Heidi was bent over the table, snorting a line. Katara looked at Johnny and gave him the thumbs up. They got her, she's in.

"Now. Same spot as last night."

He nodded back to her. Without even looking at me said, "Rose, bring that out here."

"OK baby, gimme a minute." I heard rustling and drawers open and then, a gun being cocked.

"James filled me in on how it went down, he ain't here now he finta handle other business. So Rose'll be watching over the deal make sure your boy or you"—he pointed his finger into my chest—"don't do no dumb shit."

She came out with the cash in one hand and a gun in the other. This was not the same girl who I was fucking last night.

"What's that?" I asked, pointing to the gun.

"That is a Beretta. And that bitch no how to use it. That bitch will put a bullet in your trick ass, you decide to get stupid or go running. I ain't letting 12G float out of here on a cracka promise."

We walked out into the hot afternoon California sun to the clubhouse. Rose was about ten feet behind me. I thought about skateboarding, being at the beach, or just bike riding. Suddenly I felt sad.

I shook it off as we approached the clubhouse. We walked through. I went to the TV room and Rose slipped back and waited. I walked in. *General Hospital* was on the screen. The chairs were empty, except the last row, where Eli sat. As I walked up the short stairway, I pulled out the money. I opened my mouth to say something. He put his fingers to his lips. I nodded.

I sat down next to him. He handed me a brown paper bag and I handed him the money. He nudged me and made a *watch the door* motion with his fingers. He counted it quickly, then got up and left. I got up and went to the door all the sudden I had to shit. I looked at Rose and nodded my head toward the bathroom. She grinned and shook her head. Fuck. We walked outside, Rose was still behind me.

"I really need to use the bathroom, Rose." I felt as if I was gonna shit in my shorts.

"Well you finta wait. We don't need any sidetracks. Straight back to the crib."

We walked through the door. Rose locked and chained it behind me.

"Ya'll quick." Johnny said as he came out of the back room with a robe on. "Rose, he never went out your sight, he wasn't alone with the package?"

"Nah, wasn't no thang, 'cept he tried to go to the bathroom. He got all anxious and shit." Rose was shaking her head as she put the gun down on the table.

"Well go leave a shit then, son. Make sure you use that room spray when you finish."

"Leave?" I said involuntarily, as I walked toward the bathroom

"Well you ain't taking one, is you, motherfucker?" They both laughed. I felt embarrassed.

I went into the bathroom, quickly took off my shorts and shit and flushed the toilet simultaneously. The sense of relief was fantastic. I felt myself getting tired again. I grabbed a magazine off the counter and looked at it. *Ebony* magazine. Sammy Davis, Jr. was on the cover. My father was a big fan. He played "The Candy Man" over and over for us when we were kids. I hadn't spoken to my dad in a while, because…because fuck him, that's why.

I set the magazine on the counter and pulled out the coke I had in the bindle from Eli's. I sprinkled some on Sammy's head. I crushed it and made chunky piles. I hit it. *AWAKE! I'm good. Fuck yes.* The inner voice was so good after a blast of…anything. I wiped the residue off the magazine, got up, washed my hands. Looked at the toilet, it was clean. I sprayed Glade and the room smelled like a shitty bouquet. I never got the good-smells-over-bad-smells idea. I hated air freshener. I never even wore cologne. I just scrubbed myself squeaky clean with Dove soap and used deodorant; a couple of days later, I'd do it again.

I went into the living room. Rose sat there watching TV. I asked her what she was watching. "Shhh, that's my story, *The Young and the Restless.* Johnny in the kitchen."

I walked into the kitchen. Johnny stood over the stove. Casually cooking something in a Pyrex measuring cup. He was holding it with an oven mitt. Spinning and swirling it with has hand.

"You ever smoke coke?" He rose up the cup and had it at eye level and was watching what looked like a golf ball rolling around.

"No man, I haven't. You mean free base?" He looked at me and grinned.

"Yeah, that," he said. I heard Rose mimic me in the living room. *"Free base...."*

He walked to the sink; he put water in the glass and set it down. "You may not want to start." He walked to the fridge and hit the auto icemaker button. Put a piece in his mouth, bit down half a chunk and put it in the Pyrex. "We finta use this dope to feed a rock house down on Cherokee. There a dude running shit there, he been a partner of mine for a minute. I can sell this shit for four hundred an eight, cooked up. We triple our money back. Then he fuck wit it, part it out and make a grip too. Everybody happy."

I felt myself getting drowsy. I had to get home and sleep. No, I needed to go to Bambi's. I got excited.

"Hey man, I gotta go. Maybe I'll see you soon."

"Yo, hang out. Take a ride with me later." He was putting the golf ball on a folded bed of napkins.

"I can't, man. I need to show up at the pad. My parents, that stuff." I was fading, tired and hungry.

"Yeah, I get it. Stay close, I'm a need you in a couple of days again for another one of these."

"OK, I will." I felt excitement but I concealed it. I waved to Rose in the living room.

I exited the side of his building and went back home.

As I entered I heard Danny screaming. "Go, you motherfucker! Run, run!" He was watching a football game on two different TVs. He had the volume turned down on the TVs and a small clock radio on listening to the basketball game, with Chick Hearn's voice announcing the game.

"Hey, what's up, Dan?"

He waved me off. I walked into the kitchen, opened the fridge.

"GO, YOU FUCKING KANGAROO! GO, GO!" Sometimes Danny called blacks kangaroos. He said he called them that because of the hats they wore, Kangols, and the way they walked. He yelled into the kitchen to me, "Don't eat all the rye bread and turkey meat, and don't drink all my Dr. Brown's. You eat like you got two assholes."

"I won't," I grabbed some turkey and squirted mustard in my mouth. Then I took a big swig off the gallon of milk. Everything tasted and felt good in my mouth. I was happy.

"Anyway, ya mother is bringing home Mr. Pizza, Chicken Delight, Pioneer Chicken, or something."

I went and sat in the living room. I saw a stack of new records. One of Danny's customers, Evan Charles, was a deejay at KFI radio. He always brought over a stack of promo albums, mostly new wave and punk tunes. I flipped through them. Gary Numan, The Cars, X, the soundtrack to the movie *Times Square*, and Public Image. It all looked good.

"Hey Dan, can I have these?" I picked up the stack, and started towards my room.

"Sure. Take 'em. I don't give a fuck," his eyes still on the game.

I went in my room and set them down. I went over to the record player. Richard Pryor's *Bicentennial Nigger* was on the turntable. I put it on. I loved the acid trip bit. I loved Pryor. He really made me laugh, no matter what was going on. My mom had bought me the album for my 12th birthday, 1976. That, and the *Hustler* magazine with the scratch-n-sniff centerfold. It seemed like so long ago. I lay down and I fell out.

I felt a hand on my shoulder.

"Michael, wake up. Are you hungry?" It was my mother. She was still in her nurse's uniform. She had a smile. She was a great mother. High on coke and drunk most of the time, but she still did her best.

"Hi Mom. Where's Danny? What time is it?" I felt disoriented. Still tired. I immediately thought of Bambi.

"Danny is playing cards. It's about nine."

"OK. Yes, I'm hungry. What'd you get?" I jumped outta bed and saw chicken and pizza on the dining room table. There was Coke and 7 Up. I grabbed a paper plate, started piling food.

"I haven't seen you in a couple of days. How is school, Mike?" Danny was still making duplicate porn tapes. She mimicked the audio of the porn actress in the scene. *"Ooh ah, uh uh…"* Then chuckled.

"School is good. I mean, same old stuff." I was hungry and irritated. She got up and walked over to the TV and turned it off.

"Do you go to school?"

I looked at her, my mother. I loved her, but I lied to her like I did to everybody else about everything.

"Yes, of course. Where else would I go?" She looked at me and grinned.

"Michael, please." She walked over to the freezer and grabbed her Tanqueray gin. "You have a habit of disappearing—from school, from home, and in general." She poured a drink. I hated Tanqueray. It was silent for a moment. Then I had to say it.

"OK. Yeah, I haven't been going to school." We both looked at each other for a moment. She picked up her bottle and walked to her bedroom. This was how the scene always went.

"Do whatever the fuck you want." She slammed the door behind her.

I will. I would. I always do. I couldn't help it. I tried to be good, but the bad always won. They didn't know what to do.

After years of burning things down (the backyard, my mother's bed, the garage, lots of plastic toy army men) then stealing things (various items from neighbors, bikes, and Matchbox cars, things from the liquor store) they figured I needed a psychologist. They kept it in-house. My mother was with a man at the time that operated BMI, Behavior Modification Institute. He had also written a book. *Man, The Sensual Male*, a sex primer for the wayward sexual man of 1971. He organized backyard orgies with other swingers. They drank wine and smoked grass and tripped on acid. My sister and I, just watching adults fuck. I would talk about all these things with Dr. Lichter, as well as the verbal and physical abuse my real father was committing. He would sit there staring at a legal pad. He always wore a turtleneck, he'd be smoking a pipe, nodding his head, pulling his Van-Dyke-style goatee and occasionally saying, "I see." Then after forty minutes he'd say, "Well that was great. Let's see what happens this week." It was the same thing every week.

My sister would talk back, calling them on all their lies and behavior. Then she moved out, ran away with a boy-friend who got some settlement money when he turned 18. They smoked sherm and drink Budweiser all day and night.

I sat and stared at a painting on the wall for a moment. The big-titted nude on canvas stared back. I thought about Bambi, B-106. "I got to go over there," I said aloud.

I got up and went to the closed door of my mom's room. I knocked lightly, "Mom, I'm going up to a friend's house."

"Whatever, I don't care," she yelled back. She had her same routine every night. Come home from work, grab the Tanqueray gin, blow a couple of lines of coke and read a book or two or three, every week. I walked out.

I felt my eyes well up; I pushed it way down. I still had the coke in my pocket. I went down to the clubhouse and hit the bathroom. I spilled out a couple of rocks on the back of the toilet. I took out my house key. It was on a little blue plastic *#1 Son* keychain my mother had given me. I ripped the plastic *#1 Son* off and flushed down the toilet. I crushed down the rocks and rolled up a hundred dollar bill. I snort-ed those lines deep; I wanted it as far back in my brain as possible. I felt my knees get weak as I sat down on the toilet. It worked. It took it all away. I walked up to B building. I wanted to see if Bambi could make it all better.

OPERATION: READINESS

I aimed my weapon at an aircraft mechanic who was about forty yards away. As I walked the fight line of the Alert Aircraft Parking Area (AAPA) in Plattsburg, New York, boredom was settling in. The words from a technical sergeant at basic training still echoed in my head:

"You're gonna see the world. Get an education...man, all that pussy!"

We were all yelling this the night before our orders came in; that was six months ago in San Antonio, Texas. Little did we know the exotic locations were for officers, sergeants, nieces, and nephews of the higher-ranking, not us. We were still wet behind the ears, idiots with no tenure, experience, or brains. And now I was there with my basic training comrades, drinking and drugging ourselves silly, and trying to act like Security Policemen. Plattsburg was the coldest base in the northeast, located thirty miles south of Montreal and surrounded by lakes, mountains, and snow. It was a SAC (Strategic Air Command) base, and SAC stayed on top of you like a horny drunk uncle at a family campout.

I was thinking about all this as I posted a boundary rope around the FB-111 aircraft. It was uploaded with enough nukes to take out the entire tri-state area. I stopped to pee on the plane's tires. The urine froze quickly, and looked like a golden arch in mid-air. It reminded me of McDonald's. The founder, Ray Kroc, pissed on the world and made billions; I pissed on a million-dollar airplane tire and made $572.67 a month. I looked at the thermometer on my key-chain; it read well below five degrees. The wind coming off the water created a lake chill factor that sometimes brought the temperature down 15 to 30 degrees below zero. Snot was freezing in my nose, and when it wasn't, there was the smell of jet fuel and burnt rubber. I wore protective goggles to keep from going snow-blind. I walked around the geno-cidal aircraft with my weapon at port arms. The anger, fear, and resentment of this place started to kick in, just as it had every day around that time.

My job here was to protect the FB-111s from foreign or domestic terrorism. There was also the chance that another Security Policeman would go insane and start shooting at the planes, the other personnel, the nukes, or, hopefully, themselves. What's one less of these assholes anyway? I couldn't stand ninety percent of them. They were an embar-rassment to the already ridiculous job. These people would snitch you out over anything. I mean, they would roll over their dying mother to fuck their sister if it would earn them a field promotion. I walked into the small gate shack locat-ed about ten yards from the aircraft. I took my binoculars out and scanned the other five planes, which were located in makeshift hangars. The other SPs were walking around their planes, aiming at imaginary targets, smoking, picking their noses, or looking bored. Each plane had a dedicated SP guarding it.

I opened up my duffel bag, took out my flashlight, un-screwed the top and spilled the contents onto the counter in the gate shack. There was a glass pipe, some rocks that I had cooked up before my shift, two lighters and about a gram of crystal meth. I tapped out a small line of the powder and did a hit in each nostril.

"Fuckin' invincible!" I yelled as the powder rocked my septum. Then in a mechanical movement, I loaded the pipe up with a rock and melted it into the screen.

Quickly, paranoia set in. I put the pipe down and jacked a round into my weapon, an M-16, 5.56 caliber full metal jacket, equipped with the M203 grenade launcher. I laid the weapon across my lap and took a big hit off the pipe. Buzzing and chirping sounds came from deep within my head, then bliss and euphoria. As I was letting out the monster hit, Sergeant Smithers' voice crackled on the radio:

"Airman Martin, prepare for ORI at 1500 hours."

What was that? Had I heard him correctly? I quickly glanced at my watch. It was 1445. That meant that in 15 minutes some suck-ass colonel from Washington was going to test my memory on weapons, maneuvers, and policies regarding the nukes. I took the remainder of the crystal and poured it into a Diet Coke bottle. I took three deep breaths and guzzled it down; it came up quick. I swallowed it again and kept it down. I looked at my watch, 1452. FUCK! Where did those minutes go, I need a hit. I loaded a huge rock into the pipe and hit it hard. A *wah-wah-wah* sound was the last thing I heard before my knees went weak and I collapsed onto the floor of the guard shack.

It was five degrees outside and the sweat was coming out of my forehead like raindrops. I thought about the twenty-five 10mg Valium and the flask of Bacardi 151 I had stashed in my ankle holster. I didn't need it right now, and one of the inspectors might smell the alcohol. I didn't need to come down anyway. I felt frosty, sharp, and vigilant. *And ready to kill, if I may add, Colonel.*

I made it to my feet and I looked at my watch again: 1458. I loaded a grenade into the launcher, which was strictly forbidden under the guidelines of the Uniform Code of Military Justice. If I fail this test, I'm taking them all to hell. Yes, even you, General Spit-Shine Fuckface.

I had failed an inspection before and was warned by Sargent Smithers that I would be busted down if it happened again. That was funny because I was a slick sleeve— no stripes. The lowest possible pay grade. *So bust me down*

Smithers, I'll take you to hell too! You company man, you wife beating, pig-eyed sack of shit. A nice M-16 enema, hot tracer rounds in your lower intestines. C'mon motherfuckers, because I'm done! I've had it! Please give me a reason. The resentment was thick and relentless. Then Smithers reported again on the radio.

"Airman Martin, Colonel plus two approaching your bird. Tighten it up. Cut and dry. Show 'em whatcha got. Over and out."

"Ah, fuck you Smithereens. Over." I had it with this guy.

"What was that, Airman?" I heard laughter in the background of his response. I thought quickly.

"I said was that plus two, Sergeant?" *You heard me the first time, you fat fuck.* I didn't get a response. Good. Screw him and his hobnob blowjob existence.

I joined the service to get out of a first-degree burglary/ grand theft auto/drug possession beef I had picked up coming into San Diego from Mexico. The DA was a retired Marine and gave me a choice. At some point during the court proceedings, I basically got a nudge from the judge. It went like this: Join the military, or go to jail for three to five years. Now I stood in the gate shack, regretting not going to jail. As I was thinking about all this, the voice of Satan announced himself.

"Airman Martin, report and disclose," the colonel yelled. Maywood was his name, and ripping nuts was his game. There were doodles in various gate shacks of him standing with an evil grin, holding bloody testicles, with the words, *Welcome to the SAC—now give us yours, son.* I ran out of the shack at port arms, looking at these three assholes and knowing I was locked and loaded. They stood scattered around the aircraft making small talk, about 15 yards from my gate shack. I was ready to smoke all three of them. *Who knows? I fail this ORI, they may just die.*

I ran towards them, put my weapon at left arms and saluted with my right hand, which was shaking uncontrollably as I held it out above my brow.

"Airman, prepare for Operational Readiness Inspection." My stomach turned, knowing the questions, the policies, and the anxiety and fear that came with these inspections, especially this one. I was jacked on rock, speed, and a severe lack of sleep, I had been awake for about forty-six hours. We all walked around the aircraft together. The Major looked down at the little puddle of piss, eyeing the yellow snow. He curled his upper lip and looked away.

They were all in dress blues and long wool coats. The only colors in this cold foggy gray air, except for the occasional snow flurry that carried a cherry color due to the red 24/7 lighting in the AAPA. The Colonel went right into the interrogation, snapping his finger as he asked the first question, "Airman, what is the CES?" We came up with easy memory guides. This was an easy one. Coke, Ecstasy, and Speed.

"Sir, the Code Enabling Switch, sir!" Man, I needed a hit. I could hear the cold glass pipe in my pocket speaking to me. It was getting impatient. A voice screamed in my head, *"C'mon Mike, finish up with these idiots."*

The Colonel carefully approached and looked me in the eyes. My heart was pounding, I was sweating and my goggles were beginning to fog up.

"Son, take off your goggles."

I stood at port arms holding my weapon. I could feel my index finger on my right hand slowly going towards the trigger while I removed the eye protection with my left hand.

He stepped a foot closer, looked at my forehead and then into my eyes. Shit, I was sweating and my eyes were positively dilated. *This guy knows I'm high. Maybe he gets high? Yeah.*

"Are you sick, Airman?" He asked in a disgusted tone. I thought about the damage my M-16 would do to his big head. It would explode like a watermelon, spraying brain, blood, and bone all over the others.

"Sir, you have no idea, sir." I was surprised how slowly and calmly the words fell from my mouth. I continued to look him in the eyes.

Then there was a moment of silence. "What do you mean by that, Airman?"

Then there was the easy part: lies, lies, lies, yeah. This was one of many questions that I was asked pretty frequently: *Are you sick? Are you OK, you look pale?* Or, my favorite, *Are you on meds?*

"Sir, I'm from the West Coast, and adjusting to this weather has been an extreme experience. I have had some sort of fever for the last two days. In fact, I would appreciate it if you would allow me to go to the gate shack for a minutes to grab my nose spray, sir." We all stood there, exchanging looks.

"Understood, Martin, but on the double." *He bought it, ha ha ha, the motherfucker went for it.*

I ran to the gate shack about twenty yards away, and pulled the pipe and lighter out. With my back to them, I finished what was left from the previous hit. No need for a reload. I blew it out and ran back with the *wah-wa-wah* in my head. My gun was at port arms, and I was still more than willing to shoot these clueless morons. *Can't you see how ha-ha-high I am, Colonel?*

"Let's go Airman, front and center." I was there and we saluted again. "Son, what is the Code Enabling Switch function?" This was really easy.

"Sir, this is a device that is placed on the nuclear—"

He cut me off quick and mean. "A device placed on what!" He was steaming.

I looked him in the eye, and though I wanted to spit in his face, I knew exactly what he meant.

"The *weapon*, sir, that determines the course or objective."

"That's right, son. Everyone knows there are no nukes in New York." The Lieutenant and Major laughed together about that one. I was looking into the Colonel's face; it seemed to be changing color. It was ruddy with boils, and pitted from a severe case of cystic acne. A pink-coral colored face; the texture, like a tropical beach at low tide, floating out of place in this frozen northeastern tier of the United States.

"Martin, the policy regarding the WSA?"

Whites, Speed, and Acid. I desperately wanted to tell them how I had worked these abbreviations, since half the base was on drugs.

"Sir, the policy for the Weapon Storage Area is a two-man system. No single enlisted man or officer is to be around the weapons at any time."

The other two officers looked bored during the questioning. *Bet if I fired a burst at their feet, they'd wake up!*

"Let's continue. What's a Covered Wagon Duress call, and who responds?" Oh shit, Ponderosa. Deep trouble, nukes being nabbed. What is that call?

Oh yeah, I got this, "Sir, the call is: Charlie-Whiskey-Delta, to Security Response Team #1.

This was going well until...

"OK, soldier. Present arms."

They wanna see the '16? Oh my fuckin' God, I am locked and loaded, with a grenade in the tube; that's a court martial. I guess there's room in Hell for these three after all....

I stepped back and thought quickly. It was a trick.

"Sir, I'll need to see some credentials, DD-form 622. The same goes for the Major and the Lieutenant. I will not surrender my weapon to anyone otherwise." He glared, but he knew the call.

"Correct, Airman," he said, reaching into his pocket. I stepped back, index finger moving toward the trigger, thumb-clicking the weapon to full-auto. The Colonel and the Major had produced identification, but the Lieutenant was still looking for his.

I stood there thinking of how I'd do them. Quick, three-round bursts for the three of them. Nine rounds, one fight.

Three dead. Butter Bars (the term used for 2nd lieutenants) couldn't find his ID. My heart was pounding. *I want to do them all. I bet their wife and kids wouldn't even care, just Cold War casualties. Really, really cold.*

"Sir, I left my..." Lieutenant Lucas's upper lip was quivering as he continued, "...ID at AAPA #1." His eyes watered and his face seemed to be dripping off of his skull, like clay or putty. He looked so pathetic and lost, standing there. He was chubby and out of shape. He probably never even fired any of these weapons.

After basic training, I had spent four weeks at Camp Bullis, Texas. We played war games, lived on C-rations, and slept on the ground, getting two or three hours a night. The average temperature down there was 89 degrees, with 90% humidity. Three weeks into the program, while running maneuvers, I was bitten by a brown recluse spider and my arm swelled up like a pot roast. I went to the commanding officer and asked him what I had. His response was, "Oh, about thirty minutes, then death or paralysis. Them recluse don't play." I passed out and woke up in San Antonio Hospital.

This lieutenant here didn't know shit. He was just another rich, fat, comfortable slob out of OTS. Well, Louie-Louie, guess you saved your cronies through sheer stupidity. The Colonel pulled him aside and quietly reprimanded him face to face, Lt. Lucas looked as though he was going to cry. *What a pussy.*

The Major walked towards me. He was thin, with dark circles under his coal black eyes, sunken into an almost anorexic, pale face. Maybe he smoked rock or did speed? Yeah, right. His black hair was shaved high and tight, marine-style. I immediately sensed condescension and looked down at my spit-shined boots.

"So whereabouts are you from out West, Martin?" He said with a Southern drawl.

I looked up from my boots, admiring my pressed fatigues, sharp creases on my trousers and shirt. Maybe they were sharp enough to slice the major's throat; *death by sharp*

fatigue. I could see the headlines in the Air Force news:
*Enlisted Man Goes Berserk, Slices Officer's Neck With Heavily
Starched Fatigues.*

I pretended I didn't hear him.

He asked again, "Martin, where are you—"

I cut him off. "LA, Major. Where you from, down
South?" He had a really stupid grin and looked as though he
was gearing up for a joke.

"Los Angeles...queers and steers, that's all that comes
outta there, ha ha ha."

*What the hell? Does this guy realize his life is hanging in
the balance of the LT's lost military ID? I'll humor him.*

"Actually, that's a misnomer, sir. There are no steers in
Los Angeles."

At first, the Major seemed confused with the retort; he
was looking down the fight line at swirling funnels of light
snow. Then it came to him.

"Oh ha ha, I get it. So there's only fags?"

I put my hand on my hip and batted my eyes. He looked
away from me; face flushed, and obviously humiliated. I
stood there in my pose. The Colonel walked up behind the
Major, startling him. I immediately went into port arms and
saluted.

The colonel saluted back to me and said to the Major,
"Two years in Officer Training School, and Lucas leaves his
ID on some enlisted man's post. The moron. Good job, Air-
man Martin, we will return later. Let's go, Major Salley."

The Major turned quickly and walked with the Colonel and the Lieutenant toward the control tower. When he
looked back at me, I batted my eyes at him again. He said
something to Mayfield; the Colonel looked back, and I
saluted. He saluted back and shook his head in disbelief at
the Major. So the three of them finally left. I headed back to
the gate shack; another close call neatly avoided. Now it was
time for another hit.

SLIPPING INTO DARKNESS

I **move** into a new place on Van Ness, about a block and a half south of Santa Monica Boulevard. What lures me into this unique little shithole is George the superintendent. George is a big Greek guy, with even bigger Christian beliefs.

"God brought you here, Michael," he says, while cracking the knuckles on his ridiculously oversized hands. He seems to have no fingernails, or they just fused into his fingertips. His face looks chiseled out of red granite, deep pores and framed with huge caterpillar-like eyebrows. His face is weathered like he frequently summered on Mount Olympus.

"No, my girlfriend's Volkswagen did," I say blankly.

"Very funny, Michael. You must be comedy writer?"

"No, I don't know what kind of writer I am."

We look at each other for a minute, he sees something I'm hiding. Is he psychic? Does he know what a nightmare of a tenant I will be?

"Michael, this is perfect for artist, this place is located across the street from Paramount Studio, down the street Raleigh Studio, and if you speak the Spanish language, Telemundo. Telemundo the TV station, Michael, for our Spanish friends."

"Yes, George. May I see the apartment?"

I'm between crack hits and drinks, aggravated and

semi-jonesing for something more than this, than this minute. Just then, a Latino boy comes towards us with a small black and white kitten with a fat belly and really crusty eyes.

"That thing may have a belly full of worms," I say.

George grabs the cat. "See what God creates? A masterpiece, a beautiful little creature, this kitten."

"George," I break in. "Can we look at the apartment? I gotta go." In all actuality I don't "gotta" do anything. I'm unemployed, on some bullshit disability case, and fresh out of patience for God's crusty-eyed, worm-filled little creatures.

"Yes, Michael. Action, action, the world runs on action." He says with a subtle fist pump.

"Alright," I say.

We walk up the stairs and down the hall. It smells like six different ethnic meals are burning at once.

"Ah, the authentic aroma of people cooking their native dishes." He puts his nose up to a couple of different doors. "Fantastic!" he shouts.

"Yeah, those are terrific odors." I say.

He opens a door. "So this is number 39," he says excitedly.

It's quite ugly, I think to myself. The walls are bright yellow, bald bulbs on the ceiling, and there is that cubicle cheap bluish office carpet. The walls were never prepped, just heavy latex over peeling latex paint.

"Can I see another?" I ask, disenchanted with the apartment, and my lot in life.

"Yes Michael, we have two more."

As we are walking, he stops and starts saying numbers to himself while moving his index finger back and forth. I just stand there. He's looking at me and saying numbers. I agree. And he says "no," so I disagree. I'm now completely in a suspended state of self-loathing, wondering how it all went so terribly wrong.

Then we walk. He shows me the next. It's another tiny, nuthouse-looking death hovel. It's been repainted institutional blue and has the same hideous blue carpet as the others. Then I ask him to show me another. The next one is a little small, but with a seperate room to sleep in. It also has a walk-in closet, and a kitchen with an eat-in area. It's fine. $375 with utilities included. It's twice as good as the others.

"I'll take it," I say immediately.

"Yes, I thought you'd like that one."

"Yes, so when can I move in?"

"Soon, Michael. I check with Novap, they are the company who owns this and many other buildings."

"Yes, OK George," I say as I'm walking away.

"Listen, they're a great company, Michael." He grabs my shoulder. Like I need, or he needs convincing. "They refurbish buildings all over…"

"Yes George," I say.

He just keeps talking, I look at his big Greek ham hock on my shoulder, he finally lets go. He keeps talking and I keep walking.

The next day I move in. There's screaming, yelling, and babies crying. An array of Spanish and other music whose origins I can't identify.

Perfect place to write, I think to myself. *But I will probably die here, and they'll just paint over me.*

"*Ha, ha, ha, ay, yi, yi!*" I hear a loud, Spanish cackle.

"God, this fuckin' place is loud," I scream.

Along with all the other trappings, it's so roach-infested, I sleep with earplugs, for fear of them crawling in my ears. I've heard they can't walk backwards and they just trudge forth and trip around your hippocampus.

The whole six months I live there, I binge on rock and drink every couple of days. I don't want to, but I have no choice. I try to write, to keep from going insane. I truly believe I'll die there.

THE EAGLE HAS LANDED

I walked in circles around the lake in MacArthur Park. It was the break of dawn. I slowly made out the images of some other dope fiends; no one hides at sunrise.

The birds were starting to sing. People were starting their routines. I was stuck in my routine. My ankles hurt. My feet were blistered. My head was throbbing. My fingers were numb. The jones was thick and heavy for another hit. I'd been there for three or four days smoking rock. I vaguely remember eating some street tacos and dining-and-dashing on a corned-beef sandwich at Langer's Deli. My stomach growled and my mouth watered at the thought of another sandwich.

First I needed a hit. The dude I had been scoring from said he was going to re-up. *That was hours ago. I think? Where is he? I hate this shit.* I still had some money. I had been nickel-and-dime living for days. I ran out of cash, then I hit a little lick. The day before, I deposited a blank envelope in the ATM across the street at the Bank of America. I still had about $200 of the $300 that I "made" from that transaction.

A white hip-hop dude approached me. Obviously sprung.

"You want to buy some rock, yo?" He was wearing sagging jeans and a Wu-Tang T-shirt, and moving his hands like a marionette.

"Maybe, yo." *Who the fuck is this guy? A cop? Now I'm paranoid.* We walked over to the tunnel that separates the two sides of the park.

Suddenly he turned and pulled out a knife. "Give—"

I started laughing and moved quickly with a right hook. Then I kicked him hard, and he landed on his back. I was on him. I quickly grabbed his knife and knelt down on his chest. I took the knife and held it close to his his eyeball,

"How would you like to lose an eye, yo?"

"Yo, come on man! I need a hit, just like you," he whined. He was sweaty and shaking and smelled worse than I did.

"Good. This'll give you something else to think about, yo," I said as I sliced his cheek deep with the knife. Blood squirted and it almost got on me. I jumped and moved. He howled in pain.

I ran to Bonnie Brae. I pulled the knife out of my pocket as I walked. It was cheap. Looked like one of those Army/Navy surplus store specials. It had the word EAGLE cut into the handle. *The Eagle has landed.* I said to myself. Just then I noticed a black-and-white cruiser. I threw the knife into the bushes as the car approached. Then they stopped and I stopped. I had a pipe on me. It seemed futile to run.

"Where you headed, sir?" The cop driving yelled out. He was a large man, older, maybe a Darryl Gates remnant.

"Just taking a walk, getting some cigarettes. I'm in a sober living up the street."

"Which one?"

"Royal Palms," I lied.

"Well watch yourself, this is a hotspot for drugs and gangs."

"Yeah. I'm in the Royal Palms for my alcoholism, I'm not into drugs or—"

He looked at the other cop and pointed at the dash. "Look, we don't need a dissertation on your problems."

"OK Officers, have a great day." The words felt so phony as they fell from my mouth. Honestly, I've never told a cop to have a great day. I've told them the opposite. They looked at each other, then looked at me, turned on the siren and sped off. I went back to the bushes and found the knife. *The Eagle has landed.* I said it over in my head. Coke has a way of making every thought repetitious. For instance, earlier that morning I couldn't stop thinking of the chorus of "The Bitch Is Back," by Elton John. I was totally unable to control this earworm. It was lighting my mind up with the same hook over and over.

"The Bitch Is Back." And crack *is* a bitch. A real motherfucker. Now it was "The Eagle has landed." A psychiatrist told me that cocaine was like a bad pop song. The hit is the hook that keeps pulling you back in. He also said cocaine left a blueprint on your endorphins. Much the way that gambling, sex, and sugar did. *But who cares about any of this? I NEED a hit.*

I had arrived at 6th and Bonnie Brae, and a half-dozen cholos came towards me.

"What you need, homie?" One asked me.

"Lemma get five dimes for 30," I said. I felt fearless, desperate.

"Man, fuck that," I heard one say.

"OK, see ya." I spun and walked. A skinny, short, baby-faced cholo with huge Dickies and a heavy Pendleton ran up on me.

"Yo, here you go, man." He pulled six dimes out of his mouth and broke one in half. I gave him a five for the half.

"I got to try before I buy." I pulled out the stem and put the half rock in and melted it. Then I hit it. Held it in. Slowly let it out of my nose. It was plenty fucking good. I heard buzzers, planes and birds echoing. I felt like my head was orgasming.

"That'll be fine," I mumbled. I gave him the rest of the money. *I just got 50 dollars worth of the rock for 25 bucks. Shit, that's fucking great.* I walked.

Smoking coke gets really good after a couple of days because of sleep deprivation. Also not eating or drinking anything really heightens the awareness. Melt rocks into that mix and you feel like Superman. But the jones is kryptonite, so you keep on the move. You keep the hits coming, and somehow the hits keep coming.

I was on foot. I had a car, but it was safer to walk; I could run if some shit came down. I walked down Third, creeping in and out of alleyways and doorways and phone booths to take hits. I was back. Awake. Alive. It felt good to be back on it.

I walked up Western to Santa Monica, I saw a couple of bums looking into a sewer grate. They just stood there, staring. I thought I heard a voice yelling, echoing out of the sewer. I was sidetracked for a minute. *Who gives a fuck what they're looking at?* Figuring out the shit that's happening on the street wastes a lot of time. Only if it affects me directly do I really give a fuck. It's just that shady acceptance that comes with the street; you notice, but you don't care. Or is it that you care, but you don't notice? So I walked.

I got to my street, Van Ness. I opened the front gate, and I heard screaming and Spanish music. I was home. I'd developed an an appreciation for this tenement-like building. Small rooms and apartments are best for smoking rock. Less places to stash and lose shit. I mean, don't get me wrong; I still ended up taking off wall fixtures and ripping up carpet, looking for imaginary rocks.

I had a single. A roach-infested room I shared with my girlfriend, dog, and cat. It was tight, but the rent was cheap, so I had more money for drugs and booze. Anything to check out.

Daisy, our pit bull, greeted me. My girlfriend slept 12 to 18 hours a day—chemical imbalance, coupled with alcoholism. Thank God, she was medicated past all of this reality. I sat down, broke out the pipe and the dope: fat little square rocks that were absolutely my fucking master. I smoked and smoked and smoked. The room spun. I stumbled and passed out.

Yes, the Eagle has landed.

WAKAYAMA BARFLY ROUND-EYE FIRE FACE

I'm in a bar in Wakayama, Japan. It's like the Bakersfield of Japan—it's quiet, it's country, and conservative. Not Tokyo; it's mellow. The music is American top forty, mixed decades. Music can really disturb me at times; this is one of those times. I've drank 15 or 20 beers already, but I'm not there. I can't get drunk. I'm irritated.

I'm sitting with three Japanese folks. Two really cute girls, Riae and Shuyu, friends and business associates of my girlfriend Tina. Also in tow is Yoshi, Riae's on-again, off-again husband with Yakuza ties. He has a stoic demeanor that I break occasionally with my hijinks and pop-culture references. Me, I'm tall, smooth, and bored, just a semi-ugly American with a serious alcohol deficiency. I'm waiting to see my girl. I left LAX sober, and have been drinking non-stop since I got on the plane.

I've been in and out of consciousness for days, and with beer vending machines on every corner, it's highly unlikely that will stop any time soon. Problem is, I have a ridiculous tolerance for alcohol. The beer here is weak. I drink straight vodka or malt liquor when I go, and I go fucking hard. I can't get my proper fill here. So I'm in this fucking purgatory of no man's land between drinks and wanting to be drunk. It's 11:30 PM; we have time to kill before meeting Tina at 1:00 AM A couple of foreigners come in. Judging by the accents: Australian, Englishmen, and a Latin guy who looks like Gerardo, the pop star who's responsible for that song "Rico Suave." *Now that song is stuck in my head, Fuck!* He approaches the table.

"Hey, man. You're visiting? I'm visiting, too. Brazil. I'm Ricardo. You?"

"I'm Mike, this is Riae, Yoshi, Shuyu."

He shakes their hands. Shuyu points to his jeans and gives a thumbs-up sign. He nods his head. My crew speaks together in Japanese, and they chuckle. I lean over and sing "Rico Suave" in Yoshi's ear. His eyes open wide and he laughs. "YES, YES," he says, giving me a thumbs-up sign.

"I'm visiting from Los Angeles. Rico, tell me, what can I drink to get shitfaced? These beers aren't working."

"Ah, LA is fucking cool, man. You look NY meets LA. That beer has super-low alcohol content; screw this place, man. I'm an engineer. You know, serious, fuck this place." He crosses his arms and looks back and forth angrily.

"How long have you been here, Rico?" I ask. He doesn't hear me. "Rico! How long you been in Wakayama?"

"One and half years, this fucking place. I met a Japanese girl, like a doll, porcelain face, and hair like a silk pony's tail. We go to her flat, and we fuck."

Riae and Shuyu keep looking at him, speaking in Japanese and laughing.

"Yeah?"

He continues, "Then next morning I wake up. For breakfast: No eggs, three Jap fucks kick my ass. Fuck this place."

"Really? Why?" I ask.

"Boyfriend. Fuck them. I make four thousand a month, engineer chemicals. And fuck this place!"

"I guess you can't go home to Brazil; economy is shit there, too," I say.

"Yeah, mugged four times there. Fuck that place, too, sixteen-hour plane trip home. Fuck this place *and* that place," he says.

We all laugh.

"So what do you drink to get shitty, to get stupid?"

"I be back in 5 minutes," he says.

He comes back with a shot, puts it on the table, then he breaks out a lighter.

"Here man, we light it first."

"Really? OK."

He hands me the flaming shot and without even a second thought, I rally it back. Suddenly I smell burnt hair. My goatee is aflame. My collar and neck are aflame. Riae and Shuyu are screaming, pointing. Yoshi is in shock. A Japanese woman in traditional garb dumps a pitcher of beer on me. There is another one behind her with another pitcher, like they're trying to douse a four-alarm brush fire.

"OK, OK!" I yell.

The smell of burnt hair and beer permeates my nostrils. I pat my face, I rub it. My cheeks feel like melted cheese.

"Ha Ha Ha! Fuck!"

I'm fucking wide awake, and so present it's electrifying.

"Shit," I say. "You trying to kill me, Retardo?"

"Fuck that shit, I'm sorry."

I get up go to the bathroom. The whole thing is surreal. People are starring at me, then looking away. I move quickly through the bathroom door, there is sweet, slow, traditional Japanese music playing overhead. I look at my face in the mirror. I don't feel so pretty or smooth, and I'm definitely not bored. I let out a loud laugh. *Now I'm an ugly American; real ugly.* Is this my little dose of karma for H-bombs past? The skin has melted away by two or three layers on both sides.

"I'm not a doctor, but I'd say second-degree burns, Nurse Ratchet."

"Wow," I say loudly.

A very short Japanese man walks in. "Sorry sorry," he bows, and runs out.

Fuck. My girl will understand.

I go back to the table. Retardo is still sitting there. Riae and company are quite distressed.

"I want you to take a flaming fucking shot. motherfucker," I say.

"Fuck that shit, man. I'll take one."

"And bring me five shots of that shit, UNLIT! No need wasting it with flames."

"I'm so, so, sorry man. Fuck that shit. I had no idea."

"Fuck all that, go get more,"

He leaves and comes back with the shots, gives me mine. Then lights his, thinks a minute, and shoots it back. Yoshi is shaking his head. The waitress is waiting with a pitcher of beer.

His goatee and skin catch on fire, not quite as bad, but still a feeling of assurance and equality washed over me. His lips looked a little burnt too. I was happier. If he hadn't taken a shot, I would have broken him. I rallied back three of the five shots.

"Fuck this place, I got to go. Sorry again, drink on me," he says as he pulls out a $50 bill, and puts it on the table.

"Yeah, thanks. See ya."

"Mike, so sorry," Yoshi and Reai say to me, almost in unison.

"Ah, fuck it, it ain't your fault, it could've been worse. Let's go see Tina."

We walk out of the bar and down the street. I see her. She's standing there smoking, wearing rolled-up 501s, a red tartan cowboy shirt and Doc Martens.

"Honey, what happened to your face?"

"I took a flaming shot and my face caught on fire."

"Honey, why would you drink fire?"

"I don't know. Bored, I guess."

We walk into the karaoke bar she works at. She's been in Japan for two months. A skinny, 110-pound woman playing drinking games with rich businessmen at night, making good money, drinking them under the table and flirting.

And selling jewelry she makes by day.

Being the tallest one there, all eyes are on me and my burnt face.

"Want to sing Sinatra?" She says.

"Sure, why not."

We sit and drink more. And I'm feeling great. Tina nudges me and I turn around.

"Go sing 'My Way' *your* way, baby!"

I go up on stage and the music starts. The place is packed. The look of horror and confusion on the patrons' faces is astounding. Some are shaking their heads. Some are laughing, and a lot are looking away.

As I start to sing, the crowd looks past me, behind me. I turn and to look, without missing a beat, or a lyric. There's a large projection TV with a close-up of my burnt face on it, and I start laughing uncontrollably. Really laughing, like Max Cady in *Cape Fear*. People are astounded, confused. I can't stop. Then Tina starts to laugh, and the businessmen, then everybody. I walk off the stage and they all pat me on the back. I sit down and we all drink and laugh and talk. My face will heal, maybe even scar, but I don't care. I'm drunk. I feel fucking good. So fuck it. Now, everything is all right.

Against Medical Advice

I'm in the Beverly Laurel Hotel with my girlfriend Tina. I left Betty Ford AMA (Against Medical Advice). That was a couple of days ago, I think. I'm trying to retrace those six or seven days. I know before I came here I was at the Beverly Hills Hotel, with my girlfriend and a rich kid I had met in Betty Ford. He went AMA as well. In the middle of a group he got up and said, "Fuck you, you fucking fucks." His name was Jeremy. He was from Miami. His father died in his own Lear jet accident; Lear was responsible (mechanical failure). Jeremy got a settlement of $27 million.

After he left, he called me at Betty Ford. He asked me to meet him at the Beverly Hills Hotel. He had rented a bungalow. All we had to do was show up. I packed up my stuff and left. When I got to the hotel Jeremy asked me if I could get a couple of ounces of coke, and did I know how to rock it up. Yes and yes. I called the dealer.

"Come right to the bungalow," I told him to bring me four Z's. It's that good pearly shit. He said it would be 90 minutes. I knew he's coming from Pacoima; I had some time.

Time to shop: Bacardi 151, baking soda, Pyrex glass measuring cup, ammonia, pipes, cigs, cotton balls, screens, Chore Boy, vodka, and malt liquor. Ah, the lovely foreplay of the ominous upcoming orgy that was to ensue. My balls tingled. I made my rounds. Collected my wares. Made it back to the hotel. I was farting, and was starting to gag a little. The coke was mentally on me, and the physical manifestations were happening (hard to swallow when you really need that first hit). I saw Roberto waiting in the lobby. He was a straight-up *veterano*. Shaved head. Completely tattooed from the chin down.

Creased, oversized 501s, grey Pendleton (buttoned at the neck). Crisp white Nike Cortez and fresh murder-one shades, all complimented by a gold Rolex President. He sat expressionless.

Fuck you, Beverly Hills, I thought. *We're going to christen this hotel good and evil, one fat rock at a time.*

He said nothing, and followed me. He was unimpressed by it all, and was there to collect money. We weren't friends. There was no banter, or discussion. Just trust. *Don't fuck me, I won't fuck you.* Roberto shot my old dealer Miguel (aka Happy) in the face two months ago in the parking lot of Norm's on Sherman Way. He was Roberto's homie. But he probably fucked Roberto, so he's dead. I saw it in the *LA Times*; I knew it had to be Roberto.

I opened the door. Tina was on the veranda sitting in the sun, her jeans rolled up, her shirt off, in her bra. She was trashy cute, as always. She's an artist, a wordsmith, an alcoholic, a manic-depressive, and a drug addict. Jeremy was pacing the room, sweating, unable to conceal his coke jones. Roberto stood quietly.

"Jeremy, 4 Z's, that's $3800. Pay the man."

"Wait, can we...."

Roberto cut him off. "No, the money. Now."

"Jeremy, this is a no-test, no-sample type sitch, don't waste this dude's time."

"Yes I know, but..."

Roberto got up and walked over, "Give me the money now, or I'll beat it out of you, and you won't get shit, motherfucker."

"OK, OK. Fuck."

"Man, I told you. No fuckin' dilly-dallying, dude."

Jeremy walked over to cabinet and pulled the money out of a drawer. Roberto sent a text. Jeremy gave me money. I counted it, 38 Ben Franks.

"Here, man."

"Thanks, bro." Roberto never thanked me before, but this was a good-sized order. And I was making 250 an ounce, which he will give me later. *Trust.* There was a knock on the door. Jeremy freaked out.

"Who is that? Who is, who is that?"

"Relax, youngster," said Roberto as the moved towards the door and peeped through the hole. He opened the door, stepped out, looked both directions and bent down and picked up a McDonald's bag. He walked back in and emptied the contents of the bag on the table. There was a Ziploc bag, and a small electronic scale. He put the bag on the scale.

"120 with the bag, couple of grams over." Roberto continued: "I'm out."

Jeremy: "Wait..."

Me: "Really?"

Roberto: "Damn, this dude's a trip, *aye.*" Then he went through the door.

Jeremy: "I feel like I just got fucked with no kiss! No Vaseline!"

Me: "Welcome to LA."

I broke out my cookware. I methodically put about half the coke in the Pyrex measuring cup, a quarter of that amount of baking soda and a little water. I could smell the ether base of the coke, as the combo bubbled under the heat of a homemade 151 torch of cotton on the end of a steak knife.

"Tina set me up."

She said nothing, came in from the patio. Made another torch, and started prepping Chore Boy for pipes. I was focused on the process: what had been milky water had turned clear, with a pearly white puddle of oil that was slow-ly starting to solidify.

"Jeremy, gimme some ice."

I took a spoon and grabbed a little glob of oil.

Jeremy scurried like a rat, "Here, here," and gave me a cup of ice. I bit into a piece of ice and put half in the vial of cooked dope.

"Tina?"

She gave me a big three-piece glass pipe. I took a deep breath. Let it out slowly. I put a big piece of the rock in the pipe. I lit the torch. I looked up at Tina and Jeremy. They were catatonic. Staring. Waiting. Their eyes asking, *When do we get some?*

"Tina, fix a pipe for our host, this is just a test blast, I'm putting my life on the line...ha ha." They didn't laugh.

I picked up the pipe. I exhaled. Lit the torch, and slow-ly started to pull. The coke sizzled on the Chore Boy as I inhaled. The smoke danced in the glass. As it hit my lips and gums...numbness. I shook out the torch with my right hand, and sucked the last of the smoke out of the glass chamber and into my lungs. I handed the pipe to Tina and sat back in the chair. I still hadn't exhaled. I held my nose, and tried to push the smoke up into my brain. Now my whole body was numb. Magic. A *wah-wah-wah* sound, and now the echo of Tina's voice, *"Mike, how is it...is it... is it...is."*

I slowly blew out the hit and in a quivering low voice, "Magic, baby. The eagle has landed."

She put a rock in the still hot screen. *Sssss,* it reported. I watched her hit it. Her skinny, 115-pound-frame looked defenseless against the glass ball filled with smoke. I wanted another hit.

"Wait," Jeremy said. I looked over at our wealthy host. He was letting a hit out while scanning the floor with his eyes.

"A little early for that carpet game, we got a golf ball to burn, baby."

"Wait, just let me...." He sounded like a little boy. His voice and demeanor humbled by strong rock.

"Go ahead and do your thing."

I knew I'd be there soon, tripping around on the floors and looking under doors.

I cracked a 40. I love Olde English. Actually any malt liquor, but OE has sentimental value; it reminded me of my childhood. Malt liquor was my drink of choice. It went down my numb throat, still frosted with coke resin from a horse-dose hit. The first of way too many hits, until my throat was so raw from hot coke smoke that I couldn't swallow.

Throughout this smoky four- or five-day run, rules were quickly established:

1. The bathroom door stays open, no matter what.

2. No one could come in or out of the room without group consent.

3. No phone use.

4. No TV or music.

5. Room service is negotiable, but only every 12 hours (or so?).

Jeremy kept accusing me of being a cop, till I allowed him to touch Tina's tit. She was in the bathtub, we were two days into the mission, probably two ounces smoked up, everything was blurry, I was coke blind. Jeremy said if I were a cop, I'd be super defensive over him grabbing Tina's tit.

Me: "What?"

Tina: "Aw, you're fucked in the head. Here, grab it." She rose out of the bath a bit, and he touched it. I slapped him upside his head.

Jeremy: "See, that's right. You're a cop."

"Stop with the cop shit, and keep your hands to yourself."

He was also convinced there were microphones and small cameras in the ice buckets. After Tina exited the tub, Jeremy whispered that the water be kept in the tub and all ice buckets and trash cans in the bungalow were to be placed in the full tub. This would destroy or blur the image, or muffle sounds if said devices were waterproof. I didn't challenge any of these assumptions. I was steady smoking like a fucking choo-choo train. I was also stashing rocks in my duffel bag. Later on, I was going to need to smoke alone somewhere.

I think it was on day three that I broke rule four, the "no television" edict. I needed some sort of imagery; I was aggravated and sick with the sight of the room, with Tina, with Jeremy and mostly with myself. We all agreed, but sound was to be kept at a minimum. The hotel preview channel was the only channel to be "viewed."

Jeremy raised the all-important issue of repetition, that it will be too "distracting" to have anything else on. It was priority one to "view" windows and doors other than television. Why? Because they might get the upper hand. I agreed wholeheartedly at this point. I realized that I had crossed that invisible line of paranoia. When? I don't know. As I said, it was invisible. Now couple that with sleep depravation and hunger. I think I'd eaten a small bag of Famous Amos cookies many hours before. My whole body was sore. I had issues with my neck, back (upper and lower) as well as my shoulders, arms, and wrists. I had been walking on the balls of my feet for a couple of days now, so "they" won't hear me. My Achilles tendons were aching. I couldn't stop walking around. The fear was on me like a straightjacket.

I flashed back to a very frightening situation that occurred a couple months before. I was in Jack's Hideaway (a staph-infected, fleabag hotel in North Hollywood), three days into a crack-smoking run. Just fucking gone. I was getting a blowjob from a really ugly hooker named Infinity I had picked up on Sepulveda and Sherman Way. Let's put it this way: She was the last ho on the block. As I was watching the hotel porno channel and trying to nut, there was a knock on the door.

"Oh fuck! Who is that?" I whispered to Infinity. She shook her head back and forth and attempted to keep sucking.

"Hold on, stop." I pulled up my pants, tripping on them as I ran to the door. Another knock. I looked out the peephole and it was my mother. She was standing there with a book, an *Alcoholics Anonymous Big Book*. She started reading from it.

"Michael: *Rarely have we seen a person fail who has thoroughly followed our path...*"

I started running back and forth in the room. I ran back to the door and managed to whisper, "Mom, don't. Go away. Stop."

I looked over at Infinity. She put her hands up and grinned. My mother kept reading. "*Those who do not recover are usually men and women...*"

I ran to the nightstand and grabbed the pipe. I jammed a rock in and hit it hard. I blew it out and her words were echoing through the door as the, *wah-wah-wah* of the coke rocked my endorphins. I ran back to the door; she was still reading.

"Mom, gimme an hour or two to clean up. I'll come to your house, we'll sort all this out." She kept reading. "Mom, go away or I'll call the police." I looked through the peephole.

She looked up from the book, "OK, but I'm coming back if you don't show up."

She never did. But that didn't matter; I was freaked the fuck out she'd do it again, here, now. I'd rather go to jail. Blot it out! Copious amounts of vodka and malt liquor would do it. It didn't.

Tina went to sleep in the closet and figured out a way to barricade it shut. Jeremy thought she left, so she was not allowed back in, as per rule #2. There was no group consent, he argued, so case closed. I suddenly realized that Tina always kept 10mg Valium in her purse. *Where was her purse?*

The bungalow looked like caged animals had been set free in it (I guess they had). The bedspread was over the fireplace. The mattress was up against the sliding glass window, which led to the veranda. Burn marks and soot, black streaks on the white carpeting. Just trashed. The room stunk; beer, piss, and funky coke sweat. How the fuck were we going to get out of this place? I felt trapped by the pipe and the uncontrollable compulsion to keep hitting it. Wait. Oh yeah, the Valium. Where is Tina's purse? Did she lock it on the closet with her? I slowly started looking around the room. Jeremy was tweaking on a flower vase, looking at it, inside and out; he finally gave up. He walked to the full Whirlpool tub and placed it in there with all the other questionable surveillance items. I looked under the bed, the nightstands, and the dressers—no purse. I went to the closet door—still barricaded. I couldn't open it.

I lightly knocked.

"Tina." I knocked again, "Tina?"

Jeremy looked over at me, "What are you doing? Is she really in there? I thought she left." He tried the door. He started to panic and grabbed a steak knife. He ran back and started trying to jimmy the door.

"Leave me alone, I'm trying to sleep."

"Tina, give me some Valium." No answer. "Tina, just pass 'em under the door." I pleaded.

Jeremy was confused, "Hey, if she came back in...."

"Jeremy, stop. She never left, she's been in there for hours. Please, shut up. Tina, just pass 'em under the door," I pleaded.

He shook his head and mumbled, "This is how it all falls apart."

I waited by the closet door.

"God or Tina, please pass me a couple of Valium under the door. I beg of thee."

I couldn't listen to Jeremy, or my head, or watch the preview channel on that fucking TV anymore. *Why have thou forsaken me?* Then, like an answered prayer, a small wad of paper scooted its way under the door. Jeremy was adding water to the tub and had a small pile of suspicious items that needed to be submerged. I opened the little wad of joy, three Valium 10 miligram. Pills. Sing it, Ella: *Blue skies, nothing but blue skies....*

"Tina, I really love you."

Jeremy looked over at me, in the middle of his debugging assignment, "Hey, that's sweet, but she still—"

"JEREMY. DUDE. SHUT THE FUCK UP!"

I went to the minibar and grabbed a small bottle of Ketel One, cracked it, and downed the three little saviors. Now one big hit for safekeeping. I walked over to my area. (We each had our own little area.) Mine was just like I left it.

"Thanks, Jeremy."

"Huh?" he replied, as he submerged a small garbage can. I felt a false sense of gratitude, the Valium was kicking in.

"Just thanks, for everything, for the coke, for the room, the liquor, the—"

He ran up to me with his finger to his lips, "Shhh! Shhh! Please, there are still some suspect items in the pile."

I felt the numbness of the benzos creeping up on me. I wanted to watch some porn, to see some sexual imagery —to blow out any endorphins that may still have existed. The benzos had other plans. I stood up and the room spun. Everything spun. Bliss. Then collapse, I was out.

I woke and it was dark outside. *Was the sun coming up? Did the sun already go down? Where was Jeremy? Was Tina still in the closet?* I needed a hit to clear my mind of all these busy thoughts.

Just then, a heavy knock on the door.

"What?" I yelled involuntarily.

"Housekeeping."

I looked around the bungalow. I was in awe of the absolute destruction. The carpet was filthy, with small piles of lint and crumbs situated about. The furniture was turned over, soda and liquor spilled about, candy wrappers. Small broken tchotchkes, pieces of Chore Boy fused into the carpet. The place needed a cleaning, but I couldn't let her in. I don't know why this was such a dilemma for me.

"Not now, come back later," I yelled, my own voice triggering anxiety and panic in my drug- and alcohol-worn body. *Where is that fucking pipe?*

She kept knocking and repeating "Housekeeping" like a broken record.

"Housekeeping, Housekeeping, Housekeeping...."

I SPEECHLESS

I couldn't speak. My jaw was wired shut. When I did talk it looked and sounded like a ventriloquist, speaking through a harmonica. My guess was that the years of being outspoken and opinionated finally caught up with me. That karma came in the form of a blindsided sucker punch. The scenario: I had been debating with a friend in front of a tattoo shop about the Motown CD box set versus the Stax/Volt CD box set. My remark about the Motown box set as being "cracker shit" had fallen within earshot of a big peckerwood ex-con, fresh out of the Special Housing Unit at Pelican Bay Prison. Next thing I knew, I was on the concrete with a mouthful of blood, feeling around the inside of my mouth with my tongue. Loose teeth: two or three of them.

The sucker puncher asked me if I had a problem with white people, and added that he was white. He stood over me with his henchman, another shaved-head Hitler wet dream. I knew better then to make any stupid moves. He walked away. A pussy move, but lethal nonetheless. My friend helped me up and explained the white-power prisoner behavior. I was apparently lucky that he hadn't shanked me in the neck. My friend also offered me a ride to the hospital, but I declined and drove myself.

Sensing that I was going to have my jaw wired shut, I needed time alone to decompress. I had a .380 at home, but considered the many times I had socked somebody. I had also sucker punched a couple of people over the years.

I drove to the hospital and cursed, loathing my sheer ignorance, and all of humanity. I screamed and yelled in a Tourettes-like fashion, cursing my own stupidity and that of the common man.

"Fucking motherfuck shit asshole cocksucking punk trash Aryan fuckhead nazi dumbass." I did this up until I got to Midway Hospital's emergency room. I waited. Then they X-rayed. My assumptions were correct. My jaw was broken in three places. Apparently it only takes five pounds of pressure to break your jaw if your mouth is open. That right there was a good enough reason for me to shut the fuck up.

After four weeks on disability with my jaw still wired, I went back to work. I was fearful of going back to work without my voice, but I was equally bored with daytime television and the constant barrage of questions regarding my wired teeth wherever I went. I loaded up my liquid diet—Ensure, V-8 tomato juice, water, iced tea—and I hit the road.

Driving my black 1960 Chevy Impala to work, I smiled wide-eyed and demonically at everyone who passed me. Somehow it seemed to help with the dread and disdain of going back to that job. Some of my fellow commuters glanced in horror at my shiny, wired-up mouth. Framed in a thick black goatee and sporting a shaved head, I guess I was a bit scary. One guy in a green Tercel was picking his nose frantically, then suddenly swerved into the fast lane nearly sideswiping a dump truck. I was wide-eyed, with shiny chrome-looking teeth, my mouth looking like that Jaws character from *The Spy Who Loved Me*. God, that's an old reference.

I pulled up to the security gate at Multicolour Film Laboratory, where I had been working prior to my incident. The guard, Rick McQueen, who I hadn't seen in weeks, had a chiliburger in his right hand and was wiping the sweat off his brow with his left hand. He repulsed me, the meal was smeared across his cheek and a lone piece of melted cheese hanging off his chin was swinging like a pendulum. But it was real, it was solid food—A CHILI CHEESEBURGER!!! It made my stomach growl.

He clenched his teeth and asked for my ID. I thought he was mocking me, but then I remembered he always clenched his teeth when he talked. I guess it was an attempt to be more intimidating. He had a bizarre look, and an odd body. He had a Neanderthal-like brow. His face and neck had a chiseled look, packaged in sweaty, rugged, rosacea-colored skin. Below and behind, though, he had a potbelly and a saggy, big rear end. A large, pear-shaped ass that was not in proportion with the rest of his body, like it belonged on somebody's aunt, or a supervisor at Nabisco. Some of the employees said that maybe he had taken steroids, and then didn't bother, or maybe even forgot, to work out. I agreed with these theories.

"Go ahead, chief."

I hate that "chief" or "boss" shit. It's just a superfluous, condescending endearment, shrouded in phony false humility.

"You're a dick," I said under my breath. His teeth were still clenched, and he flashed an aggravated look as he handed me back my badge. I imagine all that emotion is exacerbated when you don't work out, or forget to work out as it were. Wait, no questions? Didn't he notice my wired jaw? He always questioned everything. I wanted recognition. I wanted attention. Even from bucket-butt.

I parked and walked slowly to the building. This trudge to the laboratory was always hard. I knew when I went through those gates, and clocked in, a little more of my soul and my intellect was being sucked out of every orifice.

The sun was starting to set on what we called the black tower, a four story building with no windows, no plants or shrubbery. It looked like a jail, or a locked down mental hospital, complete with a guard gate and a sally port, they checked everything going in and out. It was located on Cahuenga Boulevard and sat aside the LA River, just a big, square, onyx-colored box. Inside the lab was extremely noxious. Smells of chlorine, ammonia, and Trichloro(3,3,3) (the same chemical used in the dry-cleaning process, and also to clean barnacles off the hulls of ships) consistently filled the air. A lot of these chemicals were dumped into the LA River after dark. The chemicals were spoken about in hushed tones around the commissary and smoking areas; talk of cancer, birth defects, impotence, and sudden death was rampant. The poisonous fumes dried out my sinuses, made my lungs ache and my breathing short. They gave my skin, mostly on my face, an oily, slick texture.

With all of this in mind, I clocked in and headed upstairs to the Positive Assembly Department. It was pretty quiet, and morgue-like. Brightly lit and shining with stainless steal and polished metal, it carried a Chinese-water-torture-like hum. This department had two functions: getting the dailies broken down from the day's shoots, and sending them to the Timing Department for color correction and to the Negative Assembly Department. Dailies seemed to come in on graveyard more frequently than the other shifts. And with a skeleton crew (two people), the work never ceased. The department's other function was prepping finished features for theaters nationwide, splicing in trailers for upcoming films, end credits, and scenes that were added at the last minute.

I put my liquid lunch in the small ice chest in my locker. My stomach continued to turn with anxiety as I approached the department. Marie, graveyard shift boss, was sitting on the workbench between two stacks of of plastic film spools, breaking down dailies.

She used two old-fashioned hand-crank reels to rewind and reload the film. She looked up at me, her face bunched up like a raccoon, squinting through horn-rimmed glasses. After a nod she went back to her work. *Really? Not even a how are you, what happen to your jaw, how ya been?* There was rarely any salutation or inquiry from Marie. I guess it was for the best.

Marie had salt-and-pepper hair and a short, forties-style do. She was always battling some skin condition on her face and arms, psoriasis or a rash—which I'm sure was a result of decades of working with the film and chemicals. She rubbed her face constantly. Marie stood a little over five-feet-tall and weighed about 240, give or take ten pounds. This created physical problems—swollen ankles, knee pain, lower back and lumbar issues. These were medical conditions Marie shared with me quite frequently and blamed them all on a thyroid problem that was pre-existing, so her insurance would not cover the "twenty-five-thousand-dollar weight-loss operation," as she referred to it. Marie had been in the industry 39 years and was constantly bragging about it. She talked of the "golden years" at Metro-Goldwyn-Mayer. She continually reminisced of the thrilling excitement and the love for the all-important job. But of course, like with anything, it's changed, and not for the best.

There really aren't any glamorous jobs in post production. But based on the lie that there is, well this was probably the lowest on the glamour scale. It was down there with most of the production-assistant jobs I'd had. The paycheck was the difference; the lab was a union job, good hourly pay, medical benefits, and a pension if I decided to become a twenty-fiver. Those were people who have worked in the industry for that many years or more. The twenty-fivers wore stretch pants, or oversized jeans, suspenders, legwarmers, big sweatshirts (to cover fat bottoms from almost a quarter century of consuming greasy, second-rate commissary food, coupled with a sedentary lifestyle).

They wore belts that held scissors, mini mag lights, magnifying glasses, and pens, all kinds of pens. Sharpies, magic markers and ballpoints. It was humiliating enough to wear a badge, I wasn't wearing one of those belts. I was constantly

borrowing other people's scissors and pens and so on. Marie
was always saying that I should get the belt, and if it were
up to her, it would be a union bylaw that all lab workers had
these special belts.

I heard the drone of high-speed developers in the next
room and suddenly wished I was in there. The only other
sound in our department was the electric film reels on the
bench and the occasional sound of a film splicer.

"Sorry, no radios," remarked Marie, when she tried to
confiscate my Walkman upon employment. These quiet,
intimate moments with Marie made me uncomfortable, like
a boy whose been forced to spend evening after evening
playing charades or Parcheesi with his grandmother. Except
we had nothing in common; even when I could speak, we
rarely spoke. I guess it was the 30-year age difference. Also,
she was extremely religious. I'm not religious, like, at all.
This deafening silence went on for roughly two hours. She
was giving me that quizzical raccoon look every so often.

This is gonna be a long night, I thought.

We were cutting and numbering the evening rushes.
After about two hours, Marie asked me a question.

"Mike, you're a Jew...right?"

It looked like her upper lip curled slightly as she said
Jew. All I could do was put my hand up and give her that
sort of slicing hand motion and a hum-like response. I
mean, technically, I wasn't Jewish. My mother is Irish, and
my father is a Romanian Jew, who occasionally practiced
the religion. My response was weak and noncommittal.

She sat and shook her head slowly back and forth with
a look of pure curiosity and asked, "Well, why didn't the
Jews just run away?" Her voice was little and cartoon-like.
"I mean if there was a small group of them, well, sure, that
would be a horse of a different color." It was a term Marie
used frequently; to this day I still have no idea what the fuck
that even means.

I sat and looked at her, dumbfounded. She stood up and

continued speaking while making a strange motion with her hands, as if she were spinning some invisible crystal ball that carried the secrets of the terminated Jews. Then with her right hand, she grabbed a big silver cross that hung around her neck, looking at it while making a fist with her left hand, opening it quickly as if she were conducting a magic trick.

"I mean as a collective, as a big group, surely they could have just run away, especially a couple of million at once, storm the gates, that sort of thing.... I mean... right?" She was serious, sincere, and seemed desperate to make her point.

I looked at the dailies. I held them up to the bright fluorescent light. The ten or 12 frames I viewed were that of hideously emaciated nude people walking in circles in the snow. It was a black and white film, which was meant to look old. I knew what film it was, I had read about it in *Variety*, *The Hollywood Reporter* and some of the other film trade mags. I looked at the camera report, paperwork that came with the dailies. The film was titled *Schindler's List*. It was to be the latest Holocaust film that Hollywood had to offer. As the saying goes, "Never Forget." Marie didn't forget, and she had questions. These dailies were sparking controversy around the lab, but this was the first time I heard this theory or question. The answer was in my head.

WHY DIDN'T THEY ALL JUST RUN AWAY!? YOU MIDGET, ABLE-TO-WALK-UPRIGHT, PYGMY, CHRIST-LOVING COW! THE AMERICAN INDIANS, JUST RUN AWAY! THE ARMENIANS, JUST RUN AWAY! THE CAMBODIANS AND THE RUSSIANS AND THE EAST TIMORESE...YEAH, JUST RUN AWAY.

I sat back with my elbow on the cutting bench. I rubbed my temples, looking up at the shelves of film, cores, tape, suddenly regretting not staying on disability. I thought about that. Day after day, I would torture myself and watch the food channel. I would liquefy Entenmann's cakes and

In-N-Out cheeseburgers. Ragu with turkey meat and ched-
dar cheese was one of my favorites. I also made Soma, Vicodin and Xanax smoothies. I went through three blenders in
the nine weeks my jaw was shut.

I would nod off into TV-land, literally. I really enjoyed
All in the Family and accepted Archie, but related more
to Michael Stivic. I found it hard to accept or understand
Marie. I was a wire-jawed Meathead. I missed daytime TV
already. Maybe I could run home and watch The History
Channel, and write Marie a full report on Why The Jews
Didn't Just Run Away.

I looked down at the floor, shiny white linoleum with
pieces of film and random pieces of plastic tape used to
keep the film from unraveling. *God, I know you had to turn
your head on the six million Jews, but please, keep me from
unraveling on this ignorant old fool, Marie.*

I got up out of my chair and walked to the other side of
the film bench. I stopped and looked at the piles of film on
the shelves. I stood there diddling with the film, thinking
of how strong the polyester-based film was. Then I had a
horrible yet satisfying thought: The film would work well
in tying Miss Tolerance to the closest film truck and rolling
her down a flight of stairs while asking, *"Gee Marie, why
didn't you just run away? Why didn't you just run away?"* I
stood there looking at her, blankly.

"Do you want to go to lunch now, Mike?"

I nodded my head up and down.

"OK, be back at twelve o'clock. Mike, I still don't know
why they didn't just run..." her voice trailed off as I exited
the room as quickly as possible.

I walked the hallway still pondering Marie's question.
The idea of lunch or dinner or any meal at this hour was
ridiculous. I was just three hours into a twelve-hour shift,
and already wanted to leave. I was living off of water, Ensure, Jamba Juice and coffee, a lot of coffee. I always felt that
hunger pang. I was never full and always alert, and had lost

twenty pounds since the incident. I also had built up a little opiate and benzo addiction—which was the only thing that was keeping me from going completely batshit loony. I walked around the lab, looking for something to fix me.

I headed toward Positive Developing, my old department. As I walked through the door, the smell of the developing chemicals immediately wafted up my nose, and the sound was deafening. The only comparison that comes to mind: hundreds of metal lawn chairs being pulled across concrete, simultaneously and continuously.

Leo, the shift boss, was all smiles. Nothing seemed to affect him. He was missing two fingers (sliced off in a developing machine incident) and lost half his foot in shipping and receiving. A real union soldier. Apparently the small tire of a forklift completely smashed half his right foot (inoperable and finally amputated). I never really got the details, but he bragged about the $700,000 settlement he got, saying, "If I had to do it, again I'd rather have $1.4 million for the whole foot." Some people agreed with him, and a lot of fellow employees borrowed money from him at ten to twelve percent interest. He was a Shylock as well as a bookie; he took bets and organized Super Bowl and playoff pools. I participated in the pools but I always lost, and it reinforced my hatred of organized sports.

"Hey Mike, how are ya?"

I gave him the thumbs-up sign.

"Your butt-buddy Eric is on the dark end."

I slowly flipped him off, in his face. The dark end is where the film was kept after it was printed and basically raw before developing. We were on the dry end where the film came off dry and ready to go, people stood watching reels of some action film come off the developer backwards at seven hundred forty feet a minute.

"Looks like a winner, huh?" He said with a clown-like grin.

I smiled and thought of how much Leo looked like a

full-grown gnome, beard and all. Like he'd come to life and just walked off the yard of some Toluca Lake estate. Maybe he did. Maybe he got sick of Bob Hope's garden, and was brought to life by the kiss of Lady Hope.

He whistled as he walked away, limping and bow-legged and kicking up his heels. I looked down to my left, then to my right. Five machines cranked away. They were ten feet high, and held twenty thousand feet of film that was pre-washed, developed, washed again and dried in minutes. They rarely broke down, and when they did, it seemed like the wet maintenance team of mechanics got them running as soon as possible. The operators just stood there looking into the monitors of the developing machines like deranged nickelodeon patrons, occasionally cutting rolls and putting up cores for the next roll. I didn't recognize any of them. New guys, I guessed.

The developing department was an entry-level job. They were zombie-like, some of them picking their asses or noses or both. I walked to the darkroom of the developer through two revolving steel doors that creaked and whined as I went through. The dim yellow lighting really fogged my vision and although I had a modified flashlight, my eyes were not adjusted. As I entered I heard a voice.

"Eric is at lunch. Who that, Mike?" She shined her flashlight into my eyes to confirm. "Sorry to hear about your jaw."

I have known Ligura for years. She taught me how to hang and splice rolls in the darkroom. An easy enough job, just hang a roll up and splice it into the end of the finished roll, in absolute darkness. I remember it being a tense experience, with her yelling and having a short temper. Now she was relieving Eric and the four other machines on the dark side. Ligura was a tough ex-crackhead gangbanger from South Central. She drove a Rapid Transit District bus before coming to Multicolour.

"Yeah, I drove that muthafuckin' Ruff, Tuff and Deadly

through the worst areas. This job…shit. Ain't no thang but a chicken wing."

She had mentioned this a couple of times around the lab. Who was she kidding? This job was painful—physically, spiritually and emotionally. My eyes were starting to adjust to the dark and I looked down at Ligura sitting at the end of the machine.

"Oh, You probably wondering why I'm sittin' on all these film bags."

I wasn't thinking about it. *But now that she mentioned it….* She was sitting on a lot of the film bags that the five-thousand-foot-rolls came in. They seemed to shine in the low light. They reminded me of big Ding Dong wrappers, three-foot-wide Ding Dong wrappers.

"Well, you lookin' down there."

I turned to leave. Ligura was notorious for these situations. An ex-crack addict, but still as paranoid as though she just took a hit. She had started a situation with another guy about a month ago. He was five minutes late relieving her from lunch break, something really petty. There were words, and she grabbed him by the ears while they were in each other's face, head-butted him and broke his nose. I still have no clue how it was she was still employed here. With this in mind, it was time to go.

"Oh, uh-uh, we gonna' talk about this."

I stood there looking at her. I kept my distance, for fear of the darkroom head-butt she had now become notorious for. My heart beat quickly as I thought of a broken nose as well as the wired jaw. *Run away, just run away,* like Marie said.

"You know, I got female problems and sometimes the smell comes up…. I stack the bags up on the seats I sit on. And I wear three or four lab coats, as to not leave the smell on the seats."

Why would she tell me this? I sat there nodding my head. I really couldn't say anything. Then she put her flashlight in my face.

"What you nodding about muthafucka'? Don't you understand my situation?" I shook my head and put my hands up. I tried to speak. But she continued.

"I tried products from the Thrifty's and my pussy's doctor. Well, those crackers dunno shit. The smells still come up, even with cologne and fresheners. My old man told me it's like putting perfume on a dead catfish."

Jesus, I thought to myself, *I wonder if he got the head-butt?* That was all I could take. *How could this all be happening on my first night back?* I felt like vomiting. Would I throw up through a wired jaw? *Could* I throw up through a wired jaw?

As loudly as possible, sounding like a ventriloquist with a mouth full of bees, I said to Ligura, "Ain't no thing but a chicken wing."

She didn't find that funny and moved toward me. I ran outta there. She was a woman who could head-butt me, or possibly kick my ass. She also may have been packing a shiv or a pistol.

"I'LL GET YOUR SORRY ASS! YOU NON-SPEAK-ING, JAW-WIRED-FROM-TALKIN'-LONG-SHIT.... YOU PICKED THE WRONG MUTHA FUCKA TO...I DON'T PLAY THAT, YOU CRACKA-LACK MUTHA...!" She was really on a roll. Then I heard boss Leo in the distance:

"Now, now.... Ligura, take it easy."

Then she started with him "Yo! Fuck that, you little dwarf. Where your hat and curly shoes with bells at? Keebler-Elf lookin', bow-legged—"

Snot was running out of my nose and my eyes watered. The hall clock read 11:45 PM. I still had time to drink my Ensure, my lunch for the evening. Sometimes it's best just to run away.

BLOODY FEET AND RED MEAT

I pulled my '89 Chevy Cavalier up to the curb. The "Like a Rock" jingle I'd heard on the radio and seen on television was playing. I laughed as I thought of my little brown four-cylinder 1989 four-door Chevy Cavalier pulling, anything. It barely made it over the hill that I lived at the base of.

I liked the little shitbox, even with its missing back window on the passenger side. Somebody had broken in. Maybe they thought I was hiding some high-end sound system? The proof of this was in the screwdriver-like gouge marks around the AM-FM stock stereo system (designed by GM engineers exclusively for the Cavalier, no cassette or compact disc player). There really was no reason to attempt to take this small piece of shit of a radio out of a larger piece of shit of a car. It reminded me of the egg in an egg in an egg routine; in the end, it's all so anticlimactic. I'm sure the thief felt a similar sense of disappointment, all that work for nothing. *Thanks, asshole,* I thought to myself.

Feral cats were now using the Cavalier as a litter box. They had ripped up the imitation Corinthian-leather-style seats. The piss was soaking into the foam of the back seats, which now smelled like ammonia or some other heavy-duty floor-cleaning product. I tried hard to keep it clean, but it was impossible to keep the cats out, due to that broken window. I couldn't justify fixing it. The repair would cost almost one-third of the total price of the car. My thoughts of breathing cat piss and shit turned to curious worry; *is this ok?* What if I was touching cat piss and shit and picking my nose, or popping a zit, or picking a scab? I couldn't count how many times I'd used a nail on my index or middle finger to clean chicken or turkey remnants from between a molar or bicuspid. These thoughts churned over and over in my head. I would put cardboard or wood over the area as soon as I could.

I was working The Club anti-theft device onto the steering wheel when I saw smoke from behind the main house, more or less in the direction of the small bungalow I was renting. I was downsizing: cheap car, cheap apartment, and cheap food. I was trying to bank some cash because I disliked my job developing film at Multicolour so much. I grabbed my backpack and quickly ran around the side of the old, gray, craftsman-style house.

"Hey Mike, what's up?"

I turned quickly and saw Paco, my neighbor. He was making his way out of his basement apartment with a large bloody platter of red meat in one hand, and a half-finished bottle of Corona in the other. The stench of dirty diapers and what smelled like Roquefort cheese wafted out of the small room and pushed me back two or three feet.

I had been in his place before; roaches scurried on the floor in broad daylight, completely fearless and adapted to the midday sun. Maybe a special breed lived in there with him. The floor was sticky, like maple syrup or soda was spilled on it, and then never cleaned. My shoes would stick to the floor every step of the way. I heard roaches scurrying under the brown and pink wallpaper, which moved like panicky flowers in the wind. It looked as if it wanted to jump right off the wall. The old pink-and-piss-yellow floral print screamed, *"Help! I don't belong here!"* There was a large bump coming up in the floor that ran lengthwise across the one-bedroom unit. Paco called it a "speed bump."

"It slows the wife and kids down," he said. Maybe there were roots growing under the building, or a problem with the foundation. I laughed to myself as I thought about how the dirt, the ground—even the earth—was rejecting the structure, trying to push it away.

Paco was wearing a double-extra-large T-shirt that was so long, it covered his shorts, or whatever he was wearing underneath the shirt-skirt. I noticed that he was limping as he made his way toward the barbecue of smoke. A Corona sat atop a picnic table, and he was leaning on it like the thing was a crutch. The grill Paco used had all the fixtures necessary for propane, but was missing the tank. Instead, his son Paco Jr. was throwing pieces of roof shingles from a pile of rubbish the slumlord deemed valuable, along with fresh cut branches from the pepper tree I was standing next to, into the fire.

"Go ahead, little man." He looked up at me and smiled. Gooey red cheese doodles were packed in his teeth and gums. The doodle dust was on his fingers, his cheeks and his nose. I thought about my fascination with fire, and burning things at seven or eight years old. Paco Jr. was about that age, and he was getting busy burning stuff, his little brown body outfitted with the latest cholo fashions. He had on an oversized T-shirt and shorts, the ever-popular Nike Cortez with the fat laces, and his head was completely shaved under the Boston baseball cap. Hell, he was on his way. He was basically a shrunken version of Paco, with more style. He too had a little pot belly, and the same round face and shaved head. I saw plastic figures, X-Men (or maybe a cheaper 99-cent store version) melting away in the hellish, cloudy inferno. The little guy's eyes were ablaze with excitement. The smoke and soot from the fire was mixing with the sweat and doodle dust on his forehead. Again, for a second, I thought of my childhood obsession with burning GI Joes and plastic Army figures, setting up a full battlefield and burning those little fuckers with lighter fluid, making the sounds I thought they would make as they went up in fames. "AAAHHH!" or "OH, GAAWWD!"

Little Paco had a pile of newspapers he was wadding up and tossing into the fire—sidearm, like an old pitcher. He kept winding up and throwing them in, kindling for the culinary disaster.

Paco Senior—or Señor Paco—snapped me out of this smoky, bloody reverie. I referred to him by Señor Paco so I could differentiate between him, his son, and another neighbor, also named Paco.

"You hungry, Mike?" he asked.

I was hungry, but afraid to eat what I saw on that grill. It was producing smoke, not flame, which I didn't believe was cooking the meat or the chicken. The grill itself was caked with soot and burnt offerings from seasons of cookouts past.

"Yeah, maybe."

I looked at him as he turned and limped back to the grill, throwing on another piece of *carne asada.*

He was really hobbling badly as he made his way back towards me. Señor Paco weighed in at about two-seventy, all fat. He had a very large belly, supported by fragile chicken-like legs. Too many pounds on his feet, maybe. I looked down in the direction of them. They looked puffy, and noticeably swollen. Both feet were wrapped in Ace bandages, over what looked like two or three pairs of socks. The ace bandages were wrapped really tightly around the upper part of the foot and the arch. I think it was some lame attempt to cut off the circulation or to stop the bleeding; it wasn't working. The tips of the socks were wet and red, and left a jagged, bloody trail.

How had I missed this before? From the door of his apartment, to the smoky grill, to the table of drinks and condiments, there was blood. It looked like a crime scene, like a murder had taken place.

Had it?

Some of the blood was fresh, a deep crimson in color. Some was turning crusty chocolate brown, like dark scabs on the concrete. My stomach turned. This feast for the eyes and buffet for the senses was a bit too much. I looked back over to the table. Stacks of tortillas, three different bowls of salsa, and dark brown, sunburnt guacamole. The brown layer on the once-green dip looked like the dried blood on the concrete; I couldn't distinguish. Flamin' Hot Cheetos were scattered everywhere, armies of ants going in and out of open soda and beer cans, and squadrons of flies dive-bombing into everything.

"What happened, Señor Paco?"

He stared at me in curiosity as I feigned my best accent. Two bloody feet and it still didn't click. Maybe he had more important things on his mind.

"Your feet, they're bleeding. You're leaving a trail of blood wherever you walk." I said forcefully.

He looked at the tray of meat he was holding. The meat was so exaggerated in color, impossibly fire-engine red with blood. It must have been food coloring (possibly Red Dye #5, the butcher's best friend), I mused to myself.

I remember seeing an exposé on Fox News targeting *carnicerías* and low-end markets. It showed butchers dyeing old brown hamburger meat and steaks, which were then magically preserved by the dye.

As he put the tray down, some of the bloody juices spilled on the ground and onto his right foot. There was an obvious color difference between the two types of blood. The blood off of the tray was brighter, a more translucent, lighter blood. I looked up at him. He was looking at the meat, then down at his right foot, too.

Was he comparing the two colors of blood?

"Oh, that. I was at a club downtown and got into an argument with some drunk-ass *ese*. He told me, *'Baile! Baile!'* I don't dance for anyone, *aye*." He sucked down the last half of a beer, like it was part of the act, and continued, "So he pulled out a little .22 and shot down at my feet. I wish he would've hit my legs, but I gotta bullet in each foot instead." He shrugged, turned, and grabbed another beer out of an ice-filled, Glad-bag-lined, white plastic laundry basket.

"Are they still in there?" I stood there in disbelief; I didn't know what else to say. My head was gently spinning. This changed the whole scene, immensely.

"Yeah, but they're only small—.22, little bullets." He opened the beer and took a huge swig. Maybe he was so drunk he wasn't feeling any pain.

Now I've seen a fair share of blood in my life, car wrecks, metal and wood shop accidents—some kid cuts a finger off on a band saw, things of that nature. I quickly went through the mental files; this was the third time this year that somebody I knew had been shot. The other two were self-inflicted.

Earlier that summer, my stepfather couldn't quite get through a radical bladder surgery for cancer, so he had decided to end it all—in the living room, right there on the couch of the condo he and my mother owned. He took a .38 and blew his brains all over the sofa and the wall. It was sad, a truly horrific situation. But it was his will, and although I didn't respect it, I had to accept it.

Sometime before that, my birth father lost his balance while changing his sweatpants. He fell sideways against the bedpost in the master bedroom of his Atlanta estate. A loaded Derringer that was in his loose fitting sweatpants pocket went off and shot him through the very center of his right foot. The worst part of the story was the fact that he was already a stroke victim, and had no use of the left side of his body. At the time, he was learning to walk with a cane. After the incident, he was in a wheelchair.

The situation with Paco was somehow so different, and it bothered me more. Was it the ignorance or the careless-ness of the situation? Maybe it was the fact that he was a father, and proving to be such a horrible example, right there in front of me.

Paco Jr. was kicking a soccer ball around, the meat was smoking on the grill. My eyes were smoke-filled and watering, and the smell of burning plastic was creating dreadlocks out of my nose hairs. Paco was drinking away, and some voice on a distant radio was telling me how to get cleaner air in my house for just pennies a day.

In a subtle tone, I looked over and said, "Maybe you should get medical attention for your foot." My mother was a nurse. I knew a little something about gunshots, blunt trauma, and emergency room situations. She had shared these stories with me all through my childhood—only because I'd insisted. I used to tell her that I might want to be a doctor when I got older, and I needed details. Now the details she once described were right there in my face.

Paco had such rampant disregard for his pain, or any kind of solution, or God forbid, a smooth recovery.

"Paco, there's a good chance you could get lead poison, or gangrene, or some bullshit infection, just from walking around this yard like that." I was gently pleading at this point. Maybe I was closer to a doctor than I realized—at least in spirit, anyways. I followed him to the grill and I fed him my mock doctor's diagnosis of the situation. He still wasn't responding. He kept flipping the raw meat on the grill.

"You like it well-done or rare, Mike?" Was I hearing this correctly? *Carne asada* isn't New York steak, London broil or filet mignon.

"Yeah, well done, well done is good."

He smiled at that response. For a second, I was flattered that Paco was thinking about my food and not his feet. Maybe it wasn't my business what Paco did with his feet. I tried to be helpful, tried to give him information. One last attempt wouldn't hurt.

"Hey Paco, do you need a ride to the hospital?"

He flipped some more meat, picked up a Corona, and

guzzled it down. Then he said it. "Sure, maybe after we eat." He handed me a pile of black and crispy meat. The secreted blood from underneath the burnt heap was running onto the paper plate.

My worst fears had been confirmed. I looked toward the table. Which sauce was the hottest? Maybe it would kill any remaining bacteria in the meat on my plate. I thought about smothering the twisted, cat-turd-looking meat with the hottest sauce on the table. I wrapped the whole mess in a burnt tortilla. The thing fell apart in my hands like a jigsaw puzzle. I took a small bite, it was horrible. The meat was tougher then leather, and tasted like melted tires. Like he had cooked it out on the street the day before, and maybe even after a day-long drag race. I dry heaved. I silently thanked the Belly Gods for bringing up that small chunk of cow.

As I was spitting the mini-chunks into a paper towel, attempting to hide myself by turning away, Paco yelled over to me. "How is it?" I had the paper towel up to my lips.

I muffed out, "Gooood, very good. You still into going to the hospital?" Maybe I'd need a visit myself.

He popped open another beer, and looked over at his smelly little hovel. "Sure, lemme tell my wife." Paco peeked his head in the door and muttered something in Spanish. He walked toward me, and again said something in Spanish, this time to little Paco, who shook his tiny head, while still throwing stuff in the fire.

We made our way toward my car, I was still holding the plate of food and wondering where to put it. Paco slowly made his way to the car, and got there as I was opening the door.

"What happened to the window, Mike?"

"Shit. I don't know. Somebody broke in, I guess. Hey Paco, why don't you sit in the back." Let him sit in the back with his bloody feet, the cat piss, and the unbearable odor, he won't know the difference. Paco got in the back seat. I looked at him in the rear view mirror.

"Let's roll, *aye*," he muttered.

I pulled down on my imaginary chauffeur cap. "As you wish, Sir Paco."

We rolled away, and I quickly realized that I had left the plate of food on the roof of the Cavalier. I noticed it slide off smoothly, and fall into the street behind us as we turned the first corner. *Oldest trick in the book,* I thought to myself, *oldest trick in the book.*

SHIT IN YOUR HAT

I had just come back from Mexico; my mother had a house there. I had gone down to eat lobster at Puerto Nuevo, boogie board, walk on the beach and just spend some quality time with her. After that beautiful trip, I got a horrible case of diarrhea.

I was so careful. I only drank bottled water and drank canned sodas. But as I was sitting on the bowl for the eighth time that day, I realized it might have been the ice for the soda. Maybe the little parasites were hanging out in the ice, the very innocent looking, clear in color, restaurant-grade ice. Restaurant grade? Was that even a thing in Mexico? The ice was a cryogenic petri dish that's sole purpose was to deliver said bacteria to yours truly. It's amazing how I always go back through the history or events of the hours or days leading up to "the runs." If I could just figure out who was responsible, there could be a lawsuit, or someone to blame or scream at. Some sort of recourse; I mean, someone has to pay. I cursed my clean time, knowing that some form of opiates would put an end to this silliness.

I drove to the Bob Hope Health Center and begged to see the doctor. Thank fucking Christ I had insurance through the film industry. What do people do who don't have insurance but *do* have chronic diarrhea? I guess they buy diapers.

I sat in the plush waiting area: big, overstuffed couches,

a coffee machine, and posters on the walls of Hollywood stars from yesteryear: Mae West, George Raft, Jimmy Cagney. I couldn't imagine any of them with the Hershey squirts. The magic of Hollywood had me fooled.

I felt shame and abdominal cramps at once, and cringed at the thought of having to live with this feeling forever, or even just for today. I scanned the lobby area. An obese woman was scolding her obese children for running amok. A man with long legs, a short upper body, and little arms paced frantically back and forth, holding his cellphone in one hand and jingling his keys in the other. A guy with a neck brace seemed able to move his neck in every direction. I just had to shit, again. I was sweating and my equilibrium felt like it was sawed off at my ankles.

Pain and discomfort has a way of bringing extreme vividness to the most mundane details, or of reminding me of things that I detest. All the sudden I hated the country of Mexico and their nonchalant attitude about everything and their—

"Mr. Martin. Room four, please," the receptionist chimed in on my musings.

I went in to see the doctor. She was an older woman with caked-on makeup and fake cheap nails, maybe the last of the Lee Press-Ons. She wore big, gold, trunk jewelry.

"How are you?" she asked.

"Horrible. My ass is leaking like a sieve." I wasn't trying to be funny.

"Excuse me?" she said with a *don't fuck with me, white boy* look.

"I have diarrhea. I feel as if I'm gonna shit out my innards. Please, help me."

That made her smile. This woman was twisted.

"Well, we can take some tests."

Oh no, is she going to shove one of those fake one-inch Lee Press-On nails up my ass? I got off the table and started to undo my belt buckle.

"No, no, I'll have the nurse bring in some sample bottles."

"Sample bottles of what?" Maybe there was some new anti-diarrheal that worked at light speed. How great, another medical first.

"Stool samples. We need stool samples to find out if it's bacterial or parasitic."

"Are you kidding me? Can't you just give me something? There must be something you can give me."

She stared at me for a minute and said nothing, then wrote something in my file. Then, with a smile: "Sometimes, well, these things just got to run the course."

"Christ, how am I going to poop into a bottle?" I knew this would get her attention.

"Sir, the nurse will be right in," she said in an angry tone.

So I waited and waited and squeezed my sphincter. I think I read somewhere that it was good exercise, increased the libido or something like that. I think I read it in some yoga magazine. In this case it was a mandatory exercise. The nurse finally came in, she was a very beautiful Asian woman. She nodded and smiled at me. I felt shame and embarrassment. I had no game right now, but maybe under different circumstances there could be something between us. I found myself fantasizing about her for a minute, nursing me through the runs and unconditionally loving me. Her bad English broke all this.

"Sir, this here what we call 'hat.' Exclete into hat three time and shovel into these small bottle with small spoon you'll find in bottle."

My fantasy faded.

"Please don't say spoon," I pleaded. "Spoons are for eating food. Pooper scooper, shit shovel, now that makes sense." I wondered if this was basic ESL material.

"Ha, ha, you are a funny man," She said as she laughed. She asked me to bring back the samples in the bottles, but not the "hat." God, do I look that stupid? Maybe?

"Why? I'll clean it really well. Shouldn't waste a perfectly good plastic hat."

She laughed and left. I rounded up the hat and bottles and ran off to the bathroom. I finished in the bathroom and as I was leaving heard the nurse and receptionist laughing. I glanced over at them and they were looking at me. I thought of the old term, "shit in your hat," and laughed aloud as I got into the elevator. What did that mean? I think my mom used to say it. She was a nurse, too. Hmm, that's something to research.

That night I laid the hat over the toilet seat and went to turd town. It sounded like a Mr. Coffee machine, the way it hit the hat; I was waiting to hear the dead voice of Joe DiMaggio, their loyal spokesperson. (He banged Marilyn, that lucky bastard.)

I took the hat and set it on the sink. I opened the Ziploc bag with the specimen bottles. There were instructions in 14 languages. "Diarrhea, an international language," I said aloud as I filled the first bottle. It stated on the bottle: *Do not let the specimen drip down the side of the bottle.* I so badly wanted to return the bottle that way; that would really piss off Nurse Ratchet.

I glanced at the instructions as I spooned the slimy turd into the small jar. The instructions said, *"Do not drink the liquid inside the specimen bottle before or after inserting spec-imen."* Before or after? Jesus! Are people that fucking lame? I got angry at common man, and the stupidity of the masses. My stomach churned and I had to go again. Could I use this sample or this load? Did she say wait? Should I clean the hat? I was so frustrated. I put the hat under the sink in the cabinet. I shit and shit; actually it was like pissing outta my ass. I had to get out of the bathroom, I felt as if my whole life had become about bathrooms and toilets.

I cleaned up and went out that night. My friend's band was playing at a club. While I was at the club, I remembered I left the hat under the sink, with the shit still in it.

"Fuck, I got to get home." I said aloud. A couple of strangers turned and looked at me in wonder. I had a new roommate, I had visions of him or his girlfriend or somebody finding my shit in a hat under my sink. Find my porn, my writing, anything, please God, but not my shit! I ran through the front door and found the hat and it looked like pudding with the funky top skin.

"Eww, fuck," I said as I dry heaved and threw the hat in the garbage outside. "Now what am I gonna shit in?"

I thought about some small bowls in the kitchen. Breakfast cereal was eaten in those bowls. No I'm not doing that. I found a margarine bowl, used that, and was able to finish. All the bottles were filled.

The next two days the runs subsided a little. I was anxious to find out hat the hell was wrong with me. I went back Monday and brought the bottles.

"It's a 10-day wait," said the nurse.

"Why?" I asked. Modern medical science, I thought.

"There is only one place in LA County that checks stools."

Wow, imagine what an exclusive job that must be. *"Honey, gonna be workin' late tonight. Bill called in sick and we got more stools than you can shake a stick at."*

"All stools?" I butt in, "Surely there's a way we can bump my stool up in line." I said motioning with my thumb. I imagined I could bribe someone with a twenty.

"Yes, all stools, sir. We will get back to you in 10 days."

"Oh, OK." I left, and never heard from them again.

SUICIDE TRUST

I got a 911 text from my mom. She's not the 911 type. I knew it was some real shit. She was a soldier. She survived home invasions, arrests, beatings (from my real dad), my sister's drug and alcohol drama, as well as psychological and emotional abuse. And of course me, my psychological theme park of bizarre behavior and drug abuse.

She also survived a couple of ex-husbands, Dr. Sigmund Lichter, the author of *Man, The Sensual Male* (Holloway House, 1970; still available on Amazon). A sex primer in paperback form, here are some bullet points:

- Your penis and what to do with it
- Creative masturbation
- What to do until the orgasm comes
- Group sex

He frequently took us to Glen Eden Nudist Colony and Resort. It was a traumatizing experience at six years-old. He and my mother also had "California backyard-style" orgies.

We lived in a house on the bluffs of Costa Mesa. The décor featured half-egg chairs, fake bear rugs and Peter Max wallpaper. The weekends featured adults tripping on acid, high on Acapulco Gold, drinking vino and sitting around in the backyard, cunts, balls, and tits fully visible. They played backgammon, listened to Atlantic Jazz or Chicago or Elton

John or Blood, Sweat & Tears.

My mother left him, and then he passed away, died of a heart attack.

For the last 20 years she had been with another kind of doctor. We called him Dr. Dan. A purveyor of porn, pills, cocaine, and guns. He was also a degenerate gambler and a part-time shylock. He was a street savvy and shrewd Bronx Jew. He was a Quaalude dealer at the Rainbow Bar and Grill, and a frequent survivor of "The A-Frame," a house known for its swing parties and orgies located at the top of Mulholland Drive, above the Hollywood Bowl. (It was also a location for shooting porno films.)

He had a briefcase filled with dildoes, handcuffs, amyl nitrate, super-8 porn films, lube, pot, Quaaludes, coke, and amphetamines. He drove a big brown Cadillac Sedan DeVille and kept a plethora of felonious items in the trunk. There were guns, icepicks, and bats. There were blackjacks and more ice picks hidden in glove compartments, door panels, and in the seats. There were drugs stashed throughout the car.

He would watch over my cousin and I while my mother was working. He would take us to gravel yards and construction sites in and around LA and San Gabriel Valley, selling super-8 porno films.

Some Dr. Dildo factoids:

- He had a shoebox filled with Polaroids of him and over 200 different women in sexual acts. Most pictures, he had a big grin or a smile. A friend or a camera timer shot these.
- He stirred sauce with his penis, Thanksgiving, 1980. Twirled his dick in the gravy boat.
- Was prone to removing his dentures at any time/ place to lick clean any foodstuffs present.
- Threw an ottoman at his roommate's tabby and called it a cocksucker.

- Rented a garage in Santa Monica and kept thousands and thousands of pills in it.
- Referred to his cock and balls as a "three-piece bedroom set."
- Told me I ate like I had two assholes.
- Called my mother a fucking cunt.
- Told me hated poor people—and that when he was poor, he even hated himself.
- Said that he would love to bring Mother Teresa to a swing party and get her into that fuck basket.
- Had cassette recordings of sex acts, and on most tapes screamed, "SAY IT! SAY IT! God is Danny's cock!"
- One of his favorite lines was, "Fuck 'em in the ass and give 'em brown babies."
- Oddly enough, Dr. Dan had the most hardworking, religious, loving parents.

Now he was 74. He had slowed down, had a clientele of customers he only dealt pills too. He made a comfortable living. I had been helping him with the business. He was recovering from a bladder cancer operation. The real kicker was, they had to take him off his lithium until he had a full recovery. Before lithium (8 years prior), Danny had threatened to blow his brains out. We knew him being off meds for any amount of time was a bad idea. So we got rid of all the guns in the condo.

Well, we thought we did…. Back to the 911 text.

I called my mother. Danny was dead. She didn't have the stomach to tell me he blew his brains out. That, I found out later. She told me to come over and grab "the stuff." As I said, I'd been helping Danny with the pill biz.

He had a loyal clientele that purchased weekly. Soccer moms, car dealers, attorneys, real estate brokers, and trust fund babies. The markup was fantastic. The pills varied in cost from 80 cents to $2 apiece. We would resell for $6 to $15 each, with Vicodin on the low end, Dilaudid on the high end, and every benzo and muscle relaxant in-between. It was a great operation. Our costs were so low, we could afford to beat all the competition. The little mom-and-pops pill-mill netted between $20-30K monthly. While I was driving to the condo, I pondered all of this. I was now the owner-operator of Dr. Dan's enterprise.

I pulled up to the underground parking I saw two police cruisers and immediately got paranoid. *"Why the fuck are those pigs here?"* I said aloud as I parked the car and walked up into the complex. The wreckage I had done there in earlier years was monumental: Freebasing runs in their condo while they were in Vegas or New York...wrecking their cars, ransacking the house and stealing money, pills, anything of value or toxicity that would take me somewhere, anywhere but right then.

I walked up the stairs to the complex. My mother's neighbor Maureen quickly grabbed me and asked me to come inside her condo. She was wearing a pink terrycloth robe and Uggs, smoking nervously. She looked befuddled and shocked.

"Where is my mother?" I asked, "What happened?"

"Your mother is putting together an overnight bag," she said, sipping a Miller Lite.

I walked out of the unit. My mother walked up the sidewalk between the units. She had on a big NYPD sweatshirt and black sweats. She also looked dazed, in shock. She was carrying two bags (a duffel bag and a smaller, vintage American Express overnight bag). *Don't leave home without it*, I mused.

A couple of the neighbors were milling about. That was strange.

"Mom what happened? Why the police, what's with all the neighbors?"

"Danny's surgery didn't take. He had a massive

coronary."

I felt tears coming. "Can I see him?"

"No. It's really not a good idea. Please take these bags and go home; we'll talk in the morning."

"Mom?"

"Michael. Please just do this. Now."

"OK."

I took the bags and walked down to the car. I opened the trunk and put both bags in. I was going to close the trunk, but my curiosity beat my logic. I opened the duffel bag first. It contained 100 or so different bottles of pills. There were: Vicodin, Soma, Dilaudid, Seconal, Valium, Xanax, Percodan, Percoset, Lorcet, Lortab, Adderall, and glass bottles of Tussionex. The Motherlode. Most of them were sealed, with the prescription labels ripped off.

I took two Dilaudid, a Soma, a Xanax, and a swig off the Tussionex. I zipped the bag shut, and with a feeling of security and confidence, pushed it deep into the trunk. Then I opened the Amex bag; there were bundles of hundred dollar bills, rubber-banded together, *10K* written on each in Dr. Dan's handwriting. 17 stacks in all: $170,000.

My first inclination was to just drive. Just go, leave all this. Then I thought about how much money I could make. I saw the end of my financial woes.

I smiled, got in the car and drove home. I couldn't drive straight home. I was starting to feel the effects of all the pills. I really wanted a 40. At 2 AM? That ain't happening. I needed some rock. I knew I couldn't go home yet. I called my girl from the car, she didn't pick up. I left a message and told her I'd be home soon. I stopped at a Mobil station that I knew had pipes, lighters and Chore Boy. I had gas and started burping—the psychological affects of crack, the anticipatory farts and gags of that first hit. I got in the car and started to nod. I got out, went to the trunk and got an Adderal. I crushed it as well as I could and snorted it. It took enough of the nod so I could get to Bonnie Brae.

I went to the same spot as always, I saw my boy slinging, and figured I might as well get a G-pack ($1000 worth). I parked in an alley and took a quick blast. I felt alive, revitalized, and ready to go home and set up shop. I drove off.

I thought about Dr. Dan momentarily, and I pulled over and vomited and cried simultaneously. What was I doing? I had been in and out of rehabs, jails, and 72-hour psych holds. I had been kind of keeping it together. Now I felt myself at the precipice of the abyss. Was I really going to go down this road again?

"YEP!" I answered aloud to the heard-but-not-seen committee debating the debauchery to ensue. I made it home at about 4 AM. I stashed the money and all the drugs, took another Xanax, and went to sleep.

Next morning I woke up groggy, thirsty, dehydrated. My girlfriend had gone to work already. I felt the despair of loss creeping in. I found the stem and the lighter and the crack. I took a quick hit, and it rattled me up. Felt good.

I called my mother, she told me what happened. Dan blew his brains out with a snubnose .38, a Saturday night special, right in the living room. I was sad. It hurt. But I wasn't that surprised. I asked her what I could do. She asked me to meet her at the bank; she wanted to put the money in the safe-deposit box. I met her there with $150,000. I kept $20K for business expenses and what-have-you; she didn't need to know. I told her to forward Dan's phone to my phone number. I was going to do this.

"You think that's a good idea?" She asked.

"Oh, sure. Pills really weren't my thing," I lied. Any mind or mood altering "thing" is my "thing."

Within a couple of weeks, I was slinging the pills. I was hustling prescriptions and procuring more quack doctors throughout the greater Los Angeles area. I was also getting new customers through my existing clients. It was a full-time job.

It came to me if I could somehow replicate the scripts,

I could make thousands more monthly. So I would make blank prescriptions in Photoshop, forge the "Greek" (prescription writing) and doc's signature, and take them to new pharmacies. Every few weeks I did this. Adding more pharmacies, more inventory, more profit. But I needed more of the triplicate prescriptions (federally dispensed medications—OxyContin, Dilaudid, Percodan). So while I was in the exam room on one of my visits, I stole 24 triplicate prescriptions out of a notebook the doctor left in the room. I knew I had to work those very carefully; each one could carry a maximum five-year federal sentence. I would mix those in with legitimate triplicates written by the doctor.

It worked. I was clearing $20–25k monthly. I kept tight accounting, and I was on the books as a salesman for one of my clients, which washed about $85,000 yearly. I started using my stepfather's accountant. He told me about Citizens Security Vault, a privately-owned storage facility that rented safe deposit boxes. It was totally anonymous. Cost: $120 a year. Box size: 24'x24'x24'. It secured my weapons, cash, inventory, and a fake identity. This was all under the name Robert Hascup.

I had grown paranoid over years of this, and I made sure I had a getaway plan. I drove a simple car, wore simple clothes, and kept the bling and consumption to a minimum. I learned the stock game and started building some portfolios. I had also built up quite an opiate and benzo addiction. The crack smoking was out of control too, but the pills were great for damage control.

(As much as I'd like to talk about my home life and ex-wife, there is no need. This was all my shit, my doing. It's best to not tag her in any of this madness, or anyone else for that matter.)

9/11/2001 5:45 AM. I was up early watching pre-markets on CNBC. I had built up a nice portfolio of stocks. As I sat at my desk, with my dogs at my feet, I crushed and snorted a Dilaudid. I had a great feeling of security and wealth.

News flash! The World Trade Center has been hit by a commercial airliner.

I continued watching the stocks. Looking at earnings, news, and info. Then the South Tower was hit. Oh man! What the fuck is going on? My biggest fear at that very moment was that I would run out of pills. If we were under attack, I needed plenty of inventory—for me, my customers, the possibility of war breaking out....

I broke out my prescription copies and my patient list and got busy. It was hours until the drug stores opened. It would be a good day to run plenty of forged scripts, at any pharmacy; this World Trade Center thing would be a great distraction. Even if the pharmacies called, most of the doctors weren't answering their phones until noon or after. *I should hustle these around as soon as the drugstores open....*

I must've written thirty prescriptions that morning. I drove around all day, back and forth to drugstores, freaking the fuck out. Taking Xanax and Soma and Norco all day, feeling completely unaffected, focused on filling every last fucking one of these bogus scripts.

I truly didn't give a fuck about anyone or anything else. Friends of my friends worked in those towers. I had my own problems, strung out on pharmaceuticals. I had to earn a living. I drove all over Los Angeles.

In public, I feigned sadness, grief, and compassion for the victims and survivors. Lies. At the end of the day I had filled every bogus script. I added 3600 pills to the 12,000 I already had. The feeling of security was overwhelming. I made it through 9/11 unscathed. I would celebrate with some Belvedere, crack and Dilaudid.

Little did I know that within a year, *my* whole world was going to crumble.

ENTERPRISE WILL PICK YOU UP

I sat in the TV lounge. I was in day three at the Passage to Promises Detox unit. The room smelled like Pine-Sol splashed over alcohol, covering junky sweat. It was decorated with posters of sobriety as well as meth, cocaine, and heroin warning posters and propaganda. The décor was institutional yellow and blue. We all sat on cheap vinyl furniture; it's easier to clean, lest some junky or alcoholic piss, shit, or vomit. In the 72 hours I was there, I had already vomited on a chair and a sofa.

I was coming off of a plethora of pharmaceuticals, including, but not limited to: opiates, benzos, and muscle relaxants, as well as copious amounts of Ketel One and catastrophic hits of crack. Clinical had me on Darvon, Klonopin, and Seroquel, and the pain was still excruciating. Pains like truck tires on my legs, drills probing at my joints, and dirty hermits breakdancing in my brain. Seriously—no profundity intended. I was looking at a flat-screen television, where a man named Dr. George (who had a frightening resemblance to the leader of the Heaven's Gate cult) was telling me how I could have whiter teeth in just days (or 11 treatments, whichever comes first).

"What are we watching?"

No answer. My lips and teeth hurt from the words passing through them. My throat felt burnt and sandblasted. My joints felt like bone was rubbing on bone.

I turned around. Six or seven men and women sat behind me. Most slack-jawed, some oblivious. One guy stared straight ahead catatonically, with a bronchial wheeze that whistled through my ears like a Category 1 hurricane. Some were sleeping. Some were talking to themselves and twirling their hair. They all seemed to have the eyes of dead mackerel. Was I in a nut ward?

"What are we watching?" I asked again.

"*Jeopardy.* What up man, I'm Mario." A raspy-throated New Yorker replied.

I watched Trebek passively/aggressively belittle a contestant. I'm in another fucking detox. I felt pain, shame, and guilt rise up like a geyser, a byproduct of all the drama I created. For years I looked people I loved right in the eyes and lied, about everything. Now they all knew, and it was all making sense to them.

"There's an NA meeting starting soon, a panel." Mario chimed in.

One girl groaned. A guy said, "Oh. Right on. Recovery. Sweet."

Then a confused girl: "What? What is that? Is it fun?"

Then a hardened dope fiend girl replied, "Girl, you really don't know? Are you even an alcoholic or an addict? Are you one of us? Is this your first rodeo, bitch?"

"Yes! No, I don't know. Rodeo? Don't call me bitch! What's a panel?"

"A panel of experts," I said. "*The New England Journal of Medicine* sends them here to cure us. Fantastic results. You'll be out of here in 90 minutes. Clean, refreshed, and ready to go out there and kick the world in the nuts."

Groaning Girl laughed.

"Oh, that's fantastic!" Said the not-so-sure-what-the-fuck-is-going-on girl.

"Yeah," Mario chuckled, "that's right. They got a guaranteed recovery method, or your money back. It's the fucking cure-all.

I laughed. I'd given up on being serious about my

recovery a long time ago. That didn't seem to work either. I was 40 years old. I'd been in six or seven different detox units, a couple of psych holds, and I don't even remember all the jails, the rehabs, and sober livings. I had yet to find an expert, or a specialist. I thought I was more qualified then most, but that wouldn't keep me clean either. So I kept trying. But I rarely followed through. *Maybe this time will be different....*

Then a tech came in, a twenty-something ex-pothead. A couple of days ago I'd asked him if he was an addict.

He said, "I had trouble with pot. It was really starting to mess up my life." Pot was never really my thing. It was definitely a gateway drug, though.

He turned off *Jeopardy*. He set up a folding table and laid out some literature. He set up a podium. It had the Narcotics Anonymous symbol in the center. "All right, guys," he said enthusiastically, "7:30. Time for the NA panel."

My stomach started turning. The tech spun my chair around to face the podium.

"Thank you, half-baked." I said.

He looked me in the eye. "Come on man, I wasn't that bad."

He walked out and another guy walked in, dressed like a cowboy. His keys and wallet chain jingle-jangled. Mario started whistling *The Good, The Bad and The Ugly* theme. Fitting, for all of us.

"That's about as original as your recovery," said the cowboy.

"Ooooo," Mario replied, with his hands in the air.

I looked him over. He wore a black cowboy hat. He had an assortment of NA chips and keychains dangling off his belt loop. He wore a gold 12-step-symbol necklace with *XI* in the center, with a matching gold and turquoise 12-step-symbol belt buckle. His jeans were skintight. The sleeves of his western tartan were rolled all the way up, and he had the muscle striation of a man who was no stranger to steroids. He had a couple of tattoos—a dreamcatcher, and skull and crossbones, a dagger with a snake curled around it. The most interesting tat was a poorly done baby's face on his bicep that said *RIP Melony*, an unrecognizable date beneath it. His boots looked like crocodile, or some sort of reptilian skin (or a facsimile thereof). He had *SFV* tattooed on his neck with twin SS-style lightening bolts. His face was cratered and bright red (possibly eczema or rosacea). He removed his hat, took his hair out of a ponytail and shook it out. With both hands, he smoothed his hair back into the ponytail and held it with one hand. Then he took a rubber band out of his pocket and completed the ponytail. He looked at the end of the ponytail and muttered something about split ends. Then he walked behind the podium. He stood for a moment and looked at all of us. He shook his head, probably realizing the futility of the dissertation. He read the steps and traditions and the format of the meeting.

"Hi, I'm Cowboy and I'm a very grateful recovering addict." His name was Cowboy. He was born and raised in Big Tujunga. His father was a Hells Angel. His mother was a runaway teenage table dancer from Downey. They met and it was love at first sight, or as he put it: "Whatever, that kind of deal." He was born a year later. He says he has early memories of trauma and abuse that still haunt him to this day, and he battles night terrors.

Mario yawned, and Cowboy trudged on. I turned around to look at the others. Some of the women looked wide-eyed and horrified. Hurricane Man still sat catatonically with his death rattle, Mario was rolling his eyes, and the *Right on, recovery* guy was hanging on every word.

His mommy and daddy literally beat the shit out of him, used him as what he called an *escape goat*. They verbally, emotionally, and mentally tormented him. Once, while watching Saturday morning cartoons, he also watched his mom get gangbanged by Hells Angels. The worst part, he said, was that she didn't seem unhappy about it.

"Oh come on," one of the girls pleaded.

He paused.

"I know, sister. It's ugly stuff," Cowboy responded softly. He took a deep breath and pushed on. They forced him to drink his own urine and tied him up in his high chair for days, where, he claims, he sat crying in his own excrement.

"Which I still tend to do," He said with a laugh. Nobody else laughed. The pitch was very well rehearsed. There were pauses for laughter and shock value. He said his dad and uncle fucked and pimped out his sister, Brittany.

He claimed that he'd forgiven them when he found out that his dad and brother had been abused—as he put it, "Some priest diddled their cocks and balls, and fiddled with their assholes." That got big laughs. He shook his head and grinned. Back to Brittany: She sold pussy out on San Fernando Road. But she's clean now. He got a little teary-eyed for a minute.

"She found Jesus Christ. She's born again. Does that whole church thing, even got dunked in a what ya' call it, a beptobismal pool."

"Baptismal, it's a baptismal pool." Mario yelled out.

Cowboy paused and then added, "Whatever. Anyways, ain't nothing wrong with born-again Christians, nothing wrong with religion."

"Oh yes there is," Mario bellowed out.

Cowboy ignored him. His sister had a child and a loving husband, an ex-*cholo* from Norwalk (who, by the way, is the regional route manager at Frito-Lay).

Cowboy'd done a lot of things he wasn't proud of as a result of his disease. Stole his grandma's checkbook, stole tit-cancer medicine from his ailing mother. Took money from his nephew's piggy bank. He said he's not gay, but he'd slept with other men—but made it clear that he let them suck his dick, only.

Mario yelled out, "That ain't sleeping!"

Cowboy looked livid, but continued to say that he did

some other weird sexual shit, but he didn't want to discuss it with all the ladies in the room. He reemphasized that all this behavior was a result of his "disease." He said he "did the deal," and if we "did the deal" we'd be able to do whatever we wanted in this world.

"Fuck, stay clean and you can be the President, or whatever," he said boldly. He had a girlfriend, they went to meetings together, they lived together and they worked together.

"We spend a lot of time together, but she has her program and I have mine." They were both doing phone sales for a multi-level marketing company, a detox powder for newly clean and sober folks, called RE-GRAB. His sponsor developed the product and had it endorsed by *his* sponsor, a retired doctor, who is also in the program. He got very serious and made a thumbs-up sign. "This shit is dynamite, Holmes. I'll see if I can leave y'all some samples."

"Does it come with a spike, some works?" Mario asked.

We all laughed. Groaning Girl laughed and said, "Ha ha, yeah."

Cowboy turned dark. "Yo! Check this out, New York. Your smart mouth and your lame, piss-poor attitude is probably gonna get your ass beat, or like, shanked or shot on these Los Angeles streets out here. You should check yourself before you wreck yourself, brother."

Mario looked him right in the eye and said, "Isn't that an Ice Cube song?"

Cowboy shook his head and asked if any of us had questions.

"Me, me, I have a question," said know-nothing girl. "What does that gold symbol mean hanging round your neck? Do they have them in silver? I should get one for my boyfriend."

"Ha ha," Cowboy chuckled. "Little sister, that is the NA symbol and my clean time—11 years. A gift from my sponsor, Big Joe." His eyes started to well up. "He was shot up and left for dead by a rival biker club. A hiker found him in a ravine in Angeles Crest. He had some amazing white light visions and a spiritual awakening. He never used again."

"Did he drink RE-GRAB?" Asked Mario. We all laughed.

"OK, I got to go." Cowboy was clearly annoyed. "I'm leaving my card if anyone is serious about doing the deal, or, if you want to be a distributor of RE-GRAB, that could be a good little day gig, make some quick coin."

I sat in a daze, mystified and traumatized all at once by the qualification. Yet it was anti-climactic, because I never heard the Baby Melony story. It was a missing piece of his whole make up. I felt cheated. Whatever happened to Baby Melony?

He rushed out before I could ask. The moaner girl whispered, "Oh my god, OK, that guy was soo fucking scary. Was any of that even true?"

The other girl asked, "What's this 'do the deal' thing he kept mentioning? He's really fucked up. Jesus, I'm definitely not that bad." She got up and turned on the TV. More *Jeopardy*.

"Fuck that hillbilly. He's full of shit. Way too much fucking information—my disease this, my disease that.... If you suck dick or get your dick sucked by another man, you're a fag. Don't blame your disease," said Mario. "I can tell you this right fuckin' now, I will not be watching another episode of *Jeopardy*, or anything else, for that matter, in this psych ward."

The know-nothing girl asked, "He has a disease? How sad. How much longer does he have to live?"

Mario stood up.

"I'm out. Who's with me?" He paced around the room, "Nobody, no takers?" He made his way toward the door. "Fuck it, I'll go."

I had plenty of money, and wide-open credit cards. I didn't come here because I was broke; I came because I was dying.

"You got a car, Mario?" I got up, still in pain. Darvon. Fuck Darvon. I needed Dilaudid, Oxy, heroin. Something else. Something stronger.

"No man, no car. I don't care." He was serious. He'd take the bus at this point.

"Well," I said, "I guess we can call Enterprise."

Mario walked up to me. "Come on man, look at you. Your lips are burnt, your eyes are sketchy and fucked, and you look thin as a rail."

"Yeah, but Enterprise will pick us up." I remembered the commercial, and I'd had the experience. It was very pleasant.

"Not at this hour." Mario said. He was right.

"Fuck it, we'll call in the morning."

We went back to our room. We split a room with two other alkies and junkies. The room was called The Swamp, and that's what it smelled like. Jarrod, a trust-fund baby, was coming off Oxy and benzos. He would just sit on the bed, nude, catatonic with a tragic look on his face.

"Hey, yo! Put a fucking robe or a blanket on, pally. We don't want to look at you sitting there like fucking, the fucking statue of David. You believe this guy? Junk hanging out like it's a fucking clothing-optional detox."

"Who's David, *aye*? Who's that, HOLMES?" Asked Felix, who was suddenly paranoid. Felix was a Prop 36 guy, a Veterano Avenues gangbanger. Ordered by the court for his stay, but also coming off a 5-year meth-smoking run. The paranoia had kicked in, and if any names were mentioned outside of people that were actually present, he freaked out a little. First night he was there, he was trying to walk behind my nightstand, claiming his son Felix junior was back there. He kept repeating, "I need to spend more time with him, dawg."

"He ain't back there, man," I kept saying over and over.

"Oh, for reals?" He would look at me, stop, and then try walking behind the nightstand again. Mario threw a towel over Jarrod's crotch. Jarrod didn't flinch.

"WHO'S DAVID, HOLMES?"

Mario started getting impatient. He looked at Felix with compassion.

"Felix, bro. Nobody, man, don't trip. Fuck, we gotta get outta here."

We all finally turned in.

Sleep came hard, and was very light that night. I was riddled with excitement and suspense. That's my mental state when I'm clean and sober and the craving and obsession is on me to get high. My body was looking forward to being well. I was looking forward to my mind being completely erased, even if for a moment. I had to blot out people that cared and the fact that I didn't care.

Finally the sun was up. It was 7 AM. Mario and me walked up to the morning meds window; I was a med seeker in every place I'd been in. I asked the morning tech, Smokey, to use the phone. He was an old Valley biker dude who seemed genuinely concerned. He had a bandana on his head and an NA symbol earring.

"You know the rules. Not till 5 PM, brother." He looked at the clock.

"Yeah, fuck all that. I got to go." It was on me, heavy and hard. It was happening no matter what. We both stood looking at him.

"Aw c'mon dawg. You're going to fuck up your detox, brother. Just kick back. You might die, Holmes."

"So be it, give us our shit. We gotta go. So let me see that phone."

Then Mario: "FUCK. I'm so tired of this *Holmes, brother* and *dawg* shit. God damn."

Smokey was shaking his head. He handed me the phone. I called information to get the number for the closest Enterprise Rent-A-Car.

"Good morning. Enterprise Rent-A-Car, we'll pick you up. And this is Simon. How can I help you?" The voice was a friendly invitation into Hell.

"Yes. you will pick me up, as rapidly as possible. I'm at the Passage to Promises Rehab Center. It's located on—"

"Yes, sir. I know where it is. We can have someone there in 20 minutes."

We walked out of the detox, through the double doors, and waited in the lobby. It was sterile, with a mild scent of Pine-Sol. The Hall and Oates song "Kiss on My List" played on a faraway overhead speaker; unfortunately, it wasn't far enough.

The area was furnished with Ikea catalogue items—couches, end tables, chairs, and shelving units packed with spiritual self-help books. They contained all the literary trappings of good wholesome recovery and wellness. I imagined the residents constructed all the furniture. Trying to put a shelf unit together while high was a nightmare. I couldn't even fathom constructing anything (let alone an Ikea shelf unit) in a sober state. That thought alone had relapse written all over it.

There was a silver plaque with a list of donors on the wall. It was mostly Jewish names: Simon and Muriel Waxman, Sol and Rita Buxbaum, Sam and Helen Titelbaum, Morty and Sylvia Gravstein. Maybe these were or relatives or friends of past patients or residents? Maybe some got clean and sober, or died loaded. It only goes two ways.

I looked down at the shiny granite floors. The room had a mausoleum vibe. It was cold and hard and seemed to welcome death.

"You should really reconsider leaving," a cute little tatted and pierced birdie said. She was a busty, lusty, sexy kitten, who under different circumstances I could definitely get with. She looked us over. Mario was wearing the same black suit he came to detox in. He held his jacket over his shoulder and stood there with his hand on his hip. He was also sporting the same white button-up Armani dress shirt with blood spots on both sleeves. The dope fiend version of

American Psycho. He tilted down his retro Porsche-design shades.

"Hey, you're Tina, right? How you doing today?"

She looked at him but didn't reply. *Maybe I'd give her a try.*

"Hey Tina, do you want to go with us? Don't let the outfit fool you; I've got gangs of cash and long credit."

She looked me over. I was wearing some blown-out corduroy house slippers, a robe over a hoodie and some Adidas basketball shorts.

"I'm not giving up my clean time for you, or anybody or anything for that matter. Thanks anyway."

Then Mario chimed in, "Oh, someday you will, cutes. Trust me. We all do." He threw his jacket over his other shoulder like he was posing for *GQ.*

"Well, whatever. Not this time." The phone rang and she answered it. "Good morning, Passage to Promises, Tina speaking."

Just then a young, sparky Mormon-looking dude popped through the door. He looked at me, then at Mario, then he grinned. He walked quickly towards Tina. He held out his hand to her. She quickly waved him off and pointed at us.

"Hello, miss, I'm, oh." He turned and grinned again.

Then Mario yelled out, "Yo, yo! Enterprise will pick us up. Is that you chief? You here to get us out of here?"

"Oh yes. Hi, sir. I'm James Haskell from Enterprise Rent-A-Car, and I hope you're Michael."

We all looked at each other for a moment.

Then Mario, "Nah, pally. He is."

Haskell's face dropped.

I knew I looked bad. Like a street person or a crackhead Howard Hughes for that matter. I felt judged and a little indignant. *Fuck this guy. How dare he.*

"Sir, will you be driving the rental car?" He looked very concerned, like he was loaning us his own car.

That question required tact and thought.

"Well sure, sometimes. And then sometimes Mario here will probably drive it. I guess it depends on what state we're in. Why don't we go and we'll figure that out at the rental office? Maybe we'll even get insurance."

As we walked out, Mario turned to Tina. "Last chance, Sweets. Come on, baby. Take a chance with us."

She waved us off, and added, "Ecch, I hate The Doors."

Then Mario: "Really? Come on, who hates The Doors?"

We walked out into the bright San Fernando sun. It hurt my skin, my eyes...fuck, even my hair hurt. I needed to get to a cool, dark room. We loaded into the minivan. I took shotgun, my joints creaking as I climbed in. The pain was starting to set in. I quickly adjusted the seat back to recline. I had about two or three Dilaudid and a half a bottle of Tussionex at home. I knew my wife was working, and she had stripped me of my keys when she dropped me off at detox. I'd have to break into the house. There was also a stack of cash I needed to get. Five or six grand, I'd stashed it under the carpet before I left. My mind was racing. Haskell broke these thoughts.

"So what line of work you guys in?"

Mario looked at me. I looked at Haskell.

"A lot of different things." I said, "A little day trading, a little writing, some pharmaceutical investments."

"And you, sir? Where are you employed?"

Mario snapped back, "What, are you writing a fucking book? Taking a customer survey? Is this some pre-screening authorization? Simply fucking put, I worked at Goldman Sachs. I'm out here trying to get off a four-hundred-dollar-a-day junk habit." Haskell sat there, eye on the road, jaw agape. "What do you do, Haskell? Besides this hustle?"

There was a long silence.

"I, um... Hey you guys aren't going to be doing drugs in our cars, are you?" He was nervous and confused.

"Come on, Haskell. We just got out of rehab." I said. "But

just in case—you know, accidents happen—like I said, we'll get plenty of insurance."

Mario looked back at me, then at him.

"What else you do, Haskell?"

"Oh, right. OK. Well, I play a lap dulcimer and I build model cars," he said sheepishly.

Suddenly I'm interested. My ears perked up, as I have NO hobbies; I had no aspirations.

"OK, that's pretty fucking cool," I said sincerely. "What are you working on now?"

"A Revell 1972 Yenko Nova." He looked proud, as if it were the real thing. He looked confident and relaxed.

"Fantastic fucking car. You almost done?"

Mario sat up and watched the whole exchange, then added, "What the fuck is a lap dulcimer, who the fuck still builds model cars?"

Then me: "Pretty fucking Zen hobbies, man. Chills you out."

Mario sat back. "OK man, I gotta say, I tried to build models, but I always ended up huffing that Testors glue."

"Me too," I said, laughing.

Haskell looked at me, grinned and shook his head very subtly.

We arrived at the rental office. I'd rented quite a few cars from Enterprise for different reasons—car accidents, or my car was in the shop for mechanical work, or doing drug deals, or just cruising around looking for hookers.

We walked into the office. The place had low energy, bad lighting and foul, thankless jazz emanating from a small clock radio on top of a beat up black two-drawer file cabinet.

Then, all of the sudden, out of nowhere comes another Mormon-looking and sparky rental agent. He spooked us both.

"Good morning guys! I'm Bill Severs, the branch manager." His teeth were refrigerator white, his eyes a sparkly

Aryan blue. His skin shined from what looked like a recent exfoliation. "How are you guys? What can I do for you?" He started shuffling random papers.

Mario turned dark, and impatient. He spoke in what sounded like a low growl, which started to crescendo. He slowly paced in front of the rental counter.

"Listen, Severs. We need a rental! Fuck! Let's skip the formalities and commence to renting! We had enough of the small talk and salutations on the ride over here! I don't know, do the paperwork! Fuck, whatever, let's do this! Get that thing washed and vacuumed! Let's get this show on the road, everybody."

Bodies started moving fast, even people who weren't involved with our rental. I couldn't help but chuckle.

"You heard the man!" I said.

The manager spoke up quickly. "Sir, please, we will help you out as soon as we're done here with these guests."

Mario rubbed his temples and slowed down his pace, walked up to the counter, "Look man, my bad. We got somewhere to be. I'll chill the fuck out. Any of you suits got a smoke, a cigarette?"

A fat woman in spandex and a double-extra-large Minnie Mouse sweatshirt was sitting with a small chubby boy with Mickey Mouse ears on. She was clearly pissed.

"Sir, can you please watch your language?"

"Yeah, yeah. Shit, sorry. Cute kid. How was Disneyland?" Then, louder: *"Does anyone have a cigarette?"*

The woman shook her head and turned away.

A cute little bubbly, busty black beauty ran from the back office. "I do," she said, and pulled out a pack of Export "A".

"Yes you do," Mario said. "And you've got class."

She smiled and gave him a cig.

"You got a light?"

She pulled out a lighter, gave it to him, and asked him to go outside to smoke it. He came up to me, grabbed my arm pulled me close.

"Hey, man, get an SUV or a big sedan. Don't get one of those faggotty little disposable cars."

I nodded my head. He walked outside to smoke. Haskell summoned me to the counter. My stomach was turning; I had a glimpse of death. No turning back, no choice. We did all the paperwork. I got every form of of insurance possible. It was a Nissan Murano, the last SUV on the lot.

We walked outside. Mario jumped off a patio chair, excited. "We got it? What did we get? Let's do it!" He was happy; he knew it was another step towards heroin.

I gave him the keys. We got in the car. I looked back at the Enterprise office. Haskell stood looking at us through the window. He looked like a concerned wife of a husband going off to a second tour of the Middle East.

"Where to, chief?"

"Take this to the next block. Go right and straight up to the 101 North."

We got on the freeway. It was packed with morning rush-hour traffic. I didn't care, but I needed some opiates to take away this pain. We took the 134 and continued to Eagle Rock, and finally made it to my house. I popped out of the car and walked up to the side gate. I went through and found an open window. My dogs greeted me as I entered.

"Hi boys."

They distracted me for a moment as I looked for the pills, the money, and the Tussionex; they were right where I left them. I ran into the kitchen, avoiding looking at any pictures or distractions, any items that could bring grief or sadness. I took a big swig off the glass bottle of pineapple-flavored recovery juice. *This is RE-GRAB, Cowboy.* I quickly pulverized a Dilaudid on the granite counter with a spoon and snorted it. I felt instantaneous wellness. I walked outside to the car. Mario looked sick, befuddled, and frustrated.

"Fuck, man. you got anything?"

I gave him a Dilaudid.

"Nice, man. is there a pharmacy? I need a spike. Can I get a swig of that syrup? I just need a little, till I get some works."

I spun off the top and started to pour it in the cap.

"Come on, man." He went to reach for the bottle. I held up my index finger on my left hand and looked him in the eye. I knew better then to give him the whole bottle.

"Motherfucker, take your hand back before I crack you in the head with this thing. I'll dole this shit out a couple of capfuls at a time. Do you understand?"

He hadn't seen this side of me.

"Bro, chill. I got it, I understand."

We drove to the pharmacy. I felt better and gripped the Tussionex like a baby holding a bottle. I waited in the car. He was in and out of the pharmacy quick, with a box of needles.

"I told them I was a diabetic, they buy that shit every time."

Everything started fading a little. I felt no pain and was itchy and scratchy. We stopped and I bought lighters and pipes and Chore Boy.

I directed him downtown. It was a quiet drive. A mission. We were at Westlake and Seventh. We trekked around till I saw Speedy, my crack and dope dealer. I asked for a G-pack of crack and a G-pack of heroin. It was in and out. We got back on the 101 and headed into Hollywood.

On Sunset Boulevard. I told him to pull over. The nod from the opiates was too much, and I had to get it together for the check-in at the hotel. We pulled over, I outfitted a straight shooter quickly and took a hit. BOOM!

"Fuck, wow" I said. "RE-GRAB!"

We drove up Sunset to the Mondrian and the valet took the car. We had only the clothes we were wearing and paper bags filled with felonious items. We got to the counter. We checked in with no problem. We walked up to the room, sixth floor. It was clean, white, air-conditioned, and overlooked Sunset Boulevard. There are flowers and welcome amenities, and a lovely bowl of fruit. *I might die here,* I mused.

Very little was said as we continued our journey into a deeper hole of debauchery. Mario shot the dope, saying how different the West Coast tar was compared to the New York white. I ordered room service and forced down a chicken club and a bottle of water. I drank a couple of minibar beers and sipped off a small bottle of Belvedere.

"We should get a couple of whores up here."

"Yeah, whatever man, sounds good." He turned up the sound on *Judge Judy* and started to nod again.

"Mario, no. Mario?"

He snapped up quickly, looked around. "Huh? What?" He slowly fell back while turning the TV down simultaneously.

I took a hit and downed a small bottle of vodka. I called the concierge.

"Concierge, this is Frankie. How can I help you, Mr. Martin?"

"What are the chances of getting some girls up here? How's that work? Like two or three of 'em? Black, white, Latin, Chinese, Indian...fuck, *whatever* as long as they're hot." There's a pause. "Hello? Frankie? Stay with me."

"I can do that. Six hundred a girl for five hours."

"Great, let's do it."

"You'll have to bring me half of the money."

"Nah, fuck that. You'll have to come up here and get it. Bring me your wallet, ID and your cell phone. I ain't sitting up here like a schmuck while you handle my cash. We clear?"

"OK, I understand. I'll come up on my break. Give me like twenty minutes."

"Dude. If these chicks aren't hot, I'm throwing all your shit down the trash chute."

I waited. Then I started smoking and smoking. It was on me, thick. I drank up what was left in the minibar. Then there was a knock on the door.

"Hey man, it's Frankie."

I snapped up. Picked up the tray, the works, the paraphernalia stashed it in the bathroom. I went to the hotel safe.

"Yeah, one minute." I opened the safe. 2-0-9-1, last four of my Social. I counted out $900, took a small swig of the Tussionex, and went to the door. I looked through the peephole. He had a tan and looked greasy and smarmy, like I guess most concierge dudes look. I opened the door.

"Gimme the phone and the wallet." I immediately said. He gave them to me. I rifled through. In the wallet were his license and a couple of different credit cards and reward cards. The cellphone was locked.

"What's the code?"

He stood there, slack-jawed.

"What's the code, Frankie?"

"Oh, 1254."

I tried it. It worked. I gave him the money. He said they were in the lobby and he'd bring them up in 20 minutes. I went over to Mario.

"Get up. I got chicks coming." He was out. "Hey. Come on." I went and grabbed a pipe and a lighter off the tray. I melted a big rock on the screen. Went back over to him and stuck it in his mouth.

"Here, hit this." Nothing. I slapped his face.

"Huh huh? What the fuck?"

"Mario come on. Hit this!"

He started sucking the stem and it really lit up.

"Not so hard..." Just as I said that, the piece of hot Chore Boy went through the stem and into his throat. It sizzled. He screamed. I started laughing uncontrollably.

He was on his feet and coughing. "Ahhh fuuuckkk! God damn it!"

"That'll destroy your nod, huh?"

He coughed the little black ball of char out.

The doorbell rang. Mario ran into the bathroom. The girls came in, they all looked hot. A busty blonde, a black girl, and a Latina. All fake tits, all done up. I paid them the balance.

Mario came out of the bathroom and introduced himself. I went into the bathroom and got stuck in there, smoking and smoking and smoking. They all knocked at the door, and I could barely speak. Always saying, "I'll be out in a minute." I was smoked the fuck out. Stuck in the bathroom of a $700-a-night hotel room with a lighter and little glass stems. The girls waited. They stopped knocking.

I wish I could tell you their names. I wish I could tell you how freaky we got. But the next day when I crept out of the bathroom, they were all gone. Even Mario.

I picked up the phone, and called Information. I called the number provided, and the voice gave me hope:

"Enterprise, we'll pick you up...."

FUCKEES AND FUCKERS

Father CARL and son MIKE are driving through the suburbs of Atlanta, looking at estate-style homes in a baby-blue Rolls convertible Corniche.

Carl is partially crippled on his left side as the result of a stroke. He's wearing a black velour track suit, a Rolex Presidential, as well as his signature diamond pinky ring. His left hand's on the wheel at twelve o'clock. Mike wears 501 jeans, white T-shirt.

CARL. *(Leaning sideways.)* I didn't take you through this section last time you were here, huh?

He clicks his ring on the wheel to the music playing: Chet Baker.

MIKE. No, looks like a poor man's Hancock Park.

Carl points at a big brick two-story home.

CARL. You'd do real well out here. $300 thou gets ya a real cock-knocker! *(Shakes his fist.)*

MIKE. Definitely cheaper than LA. At this point, what isn't? *(Says to himself as he sends a text on his phone:)* Oh, wait— New York, I guess.

CARL. What?

Carl turns the music down.

MIKE. Nothing. Just thinking out loud.

CARL. Fuck New York, place is a fucking horror show, great place to visit who wants to live there now? Fucking Eurotrash and Trumpifed to hell, it's lost it's soul, it's dark artistic edge. *(Pause.)* You, know. I'm really glad you came, man. It's good to see you, kid. I can't believe you wanted to rent a car. What's wrong with you? Fucking putz.

MIKE. *(Taking pictures with camera phone.)* I didn't want to put you out, Dad.

CARL. Put me out? You're my fucking son! What the fuck do you need a car for? I can drive you around. Besides, look at this thing. It's a fucking Rolls-Royce Corniche. Nothing but the best.

MIKE. It's just...I like to get around on my own. You know... living in LA.

CARL. Whatever. Look at this place. You should come out here, it's good for the soul. Make a move...hey!

He slaps Mike's arm. Mike is obviously annoyed.

CARL. We could buy a couple of these bullshit condo units in the city and rent them out. We could pack a lot of low-life cocksuckers in one of these houses. You could be my enforcer!

MIKE. *(Still taking pics.)* I gotta lot stuff going on in LA, Dad. A house, my yoga, my program....

CARL. Aw, c'mon that's all bullshit, I'm talking Atlanta in May, man! Bluebirds on the wing, crocuses are blooming! All that Spring Break pussy! Fuck your program. Make a move!

MIKE. *(Looking out the window uncomfortably.)* Yeah.

CARL. I got a lot of good stuff going on out here, kid. I'll take care of you.

MIKE. Let me think about it. Dad. I don't need taking care of; I'm 40.

CARL. Yeah, you do. You're in denial, still really don't know what you're doing.

MIKE. Ha ha, *I'm* in denial? Come on man.

CARL. You know, I'd love to start a charity or one of those nonprofit deals....

MIKE. Dad, what are you talking about? What kind of non-profit? Are you serious?

CARL. Yeah, you fucking kidding? A lot of money in that! You know, these save a dog or kitten things. Or maybe more exotic, like *(Feminine voice:)* "Please find it in your heart to help the giraffes of the Serengeti plains." That kind of bull-shit, these rich liberals fork over tons of dough for that type of shit.

MIKE. You're kidding, right?

CARL. Hell No! People make out fat checks to charities, tax-free! The IRS can suck a nigger dick, man! Thirty percent for capital gain...legal mafia, those fucks!

MIKE. Yeah, the IRS...I'm just starting to clear up my shit.

CARL. Fuck them! You know if they really broke it down, like a real chart where my tax dollars go, you know, I still wouldn't pay those cocksuckers!

MIKE. I claimed 99 dependents one year I was working, man, did they get me.

CARL. Well that's stupid. You should always talk to me. I know the ins and outs of this country better than a bor-der-running Third-World shitter!

MIKE. *(Laughs.)* Ha ha, Third-World shitter.... I'd rather just pay.

CARL. You know I met a G, a real mensch a couple of years

ago, before I had the stroke. He gave me a million dollars.

Mike. A G? Where was this guy from?

Carl. Schmuck from England. Yeah, he gave me a mill. Wanted to buy into partnership.

Mike. A partnership in the jewelry store? Your company?

Carl. Doesn't fucking matter. Gives me the cash, then I had the stroke.

Mike. He must have freaked out, huh?

Carl. Just listen, man. So I'm laid up in a hospital, just outta a coma. Stephen, your schmuck step brother...

Mike. Here we go. It's his fault?

Carl. Just listen to the story. He comes into the hospital, after I come to out of my stroke, wake from the coma, guess the first thing the asshole says to me. *(Pointing up.)*

Mike. I have no idea?

Carl. Not *how you doing?* Not *what can I do to help?* He says the English guy wants his money back. What do you want me to do?

Mike. You're kidding me. No hello, nothing?

Carl. You believe this asshole?' *(He turns, really serious.)* I pulled him up really close and I broke it down to him, I told him, "If you or your mother have any hand in giving back that money, I will kill you both."

He stares straight ahead at the road.

Mike. Well, if you weren't going through with the deal, why wouldn't you—

Carl. I never give back money. There were no provisions, no concessions, and no guarantees! I will not give back a dime. Nothing, ever! *(Raises his fist, the car swerves.)*

MIKE. *(Goes for the wheel.)* Dad! Keep your hands on the wheel!

CARL. *(Grabbing the wheel.)* I got it. Don't worry about the wheel. What, you think you can drive better than me? With a stroke I drive better then you!

A beat.

MIKE. He's a co-partner, right? There was no agreement?

CARL. Co-partner? More like co-schmuck! *(Laughs.)*

MIKE. He's got a percentage, or something.

CARL. Percentage? Ha! He's a putz, stupid *goyim*. We had a verbal agreement. Nothing was written. *(Turns up the radio.)* Fucking Chet Baker!

MIKE. *(Turns it down.)* Does it have to be that loud?

Carl slaps Mike's hand, turns it back up.

CARL. *(Yelling.)* I love Chet Baker, man. Motherfucker had a nasty heroin habit. Jesus he was talented though.

MIKE. Takes down the good ones.

CARL. Ah, people are weak, like you are. Heroin, alcohol. Fuck, coke.... You imagine me on coke? Feels like I already *am* on coke!

MIKE. That's where I get my mania, my manic shit, Dad. You and Mom.

CARL. Asshole. That's not mania. Your mind is filled with all of that psychological therapeutic bullshit!

MIKE. Oh? What is it then?

CARL. That's fucking drive. Get up and go! Look at me.

MIKE. Yeah, right.

CARL. You just need to pump some iron. Look at you.

MIKE. *(Looking at his arms.)* I'm doing all right.

CARL. Ha, ha, good one. You know I went to Vegas? Me and Bernie. I opened up lines of credit.

MIKE. Before the bankruptcy.

CARL. Yeah, before the BK.

MIKE. *(Growing impatient.)* Are we going to the office?

CARL. Jesus, listen! I left with $295 thousand. Fucking Vegas! What a shit show, those fucking buffets. All that spandex, plastic cups filled with pennies, nickels, and quarters.... Fucking Bernie, like a pig in a poke.

MIKE. How'd ya get him to leave? Talk about a gambling addict.

CARL. You kiddin'? That scumbag degenerate? He'd bet on two cockroaches running up a wall in the projects! I'll tell you, that motherfucker used to get these young girls. They'd suck your cock 'till your ears rang! *Oy, gevalt!*

MIKE. Yeah, unfortunately, Dad, Bernie would pick up minors—15-, 16-year-olds.

CARL. Ah who cares, it's only a big deal here…in America. What, are you working with Child Services now? All the greats had young pussy.

MIKE. C'mon! Are you kidding me? Disgusting.

CARL. It was like he drove around a van with a sign that said, "Deposit cocksuckers here."

MIKE. *(Laughing.)* Alright c'mon.

CARL. He was a real degenerate with the gambling. Days at a time, no food and no drink. Not even a cigarette or coffee. Just moving, hustling, fucking gambling!

MIKE. It's a disease. Just like drugs or alcohol.

CARL. Oh bullshit. Disease? He was a lazy cocksucker at

other times though. You know we tried to do this insurance scam at Circle K?

MIKE. What is a Circle K?

CARL. It's for people who can't afford to buy a 7-Eleven franchise. The idea, a simple slip-and-fall. All's Bernie had to do was go to the chiropractor.

MIKE. What was the scam?

CARL. So I go in there, I balance a huge cup of coffee on the counter while trying to put in cream and sugar, then it falls. I mean, I let it fall.

MIKE. Sounds simple enough.

CARL. Yep. Two minutes later, Bernie walks in, and boom! He's lying there screaming and crying on the floor like a Brooklyn yenta. Paramedics come. I mean, Jesus, what a fuckin' scene.

MIKE. Cut 'n' dry.

CARL. $39 thousand! Settled outta court. We got $39 thou walk-away money! But Bernie blew off the doctor, so I got stuck with a two-thousand-dollar medical bill.

MIKE. That shit always backfires.

CARL. Ah, it's a victimless crime.

MIKE. There is always a victim. No free lunch....

CARL. Yep! That's what the worlds made of, victims and volunteers. Fuckees and fuckers! Not Bernie, even in a wheelchair after his stroke he had game, he could still pull 'em, those little dicksuckers! Where are we?

MIKE. Going to the office. You all right?

CARL. Yep, I'm good. One night I stopped and had a little sake, got back in the car to go home.

MIKE. Shit. Good way to get a DUI.

CARL. Nope, I ended up in the Cleveland National Forest. Cop pulled me over.

MIKE. You are about the luckiest motherfucker....

CARL. Cop says, "Wat'cha doing out here boy? Don't see too many Rolls Royce or Jews out here in these parts." Real sister-fucking redneck hillbilly.

MIKE. He was cool? No DUI?

CARL. No man, I was honest. Told them I had a couple a shots of sake with my Jap food and got lost. Cell phone got no signal. Honesty, Michael. The best policy.'

MIKE. That's a riot!

They pull into the jewelry store parking lot.

CARL. One day I got in this car, started it. It jumped into gear and I was zipping around the lot.

MIKE. What? Pedal stuck or something?

CARL. Yep, went right through that wrought iron fence and up that embankment there.

MIKE. Wow, really? You're lucky, man.

CARL. $130 thousand in damages.

MIKE. To the property?

CARL. Fuck the property! This is a Rolls Royce Corniche. Insurance took care of it. It needed a new paint job anyway. Before we get out of the car, kid, I got to tell you. Out of all the woman I was ever with, your mother was the best. Top shelf.

MIKE. Really? You mean out of Elizabeth, Shirley, Linda #1, Linda #2, and Rose? Still liking Mary the best, huh?

CARL. Oh you bet! She was the greatest! Amazing you remembered all those names.

MIKE. It's like a cast of a movie.

CARL. Right! I don't have to see it. See it...I fucking lived it!

MIKE. You're fucking hilarious, Dad. I hope we can hang out more.

CARL. You got to move out here, man. Stop all the bullshit.

MIKE. It's not going to happen right now.

CARL. Your mother put up with a lot of my shit. I mean...

MIKE. Dad, really, it's all in the past.

CARL. Just fucking listen, would ya? I got to clear my conscience. I put on mover's clothes and rented a big fucking panel truck, Hal and me. You remember Hal Blake?'

MIKE. Yeah, how could I forget him? He—

CARL. Yeah, so we go in there tell the receptionist at the hospital we were removing the furniture and replacing it with new stuff. I took it all. I decorated the living room with it. Used the end tables as night stands.

MIKE. Ha ha, I heard this story.

CARL. Not from me. We scammed everybody out of something.

MIKE. So go see your local rabbi or therapist. Why you telling me? We should get in.

CARL. Hey, fuck them, I must tell you this shit. I tried to jump the train tracks in Long Beach, Long Island.

MIKE. C'mon! This one I definitely heard.

CARL. Asshole! Not from me. Let me tell it, would you? You know I'm impatient, I ain't waiting for shit. Some train full of fuckin' scumbags....

MIKE. That sums it up, huh, Dad? Narrows down the whole

passenger list?

CARL. You know it's true, coming from out on the Island. Ronkonkoma, Wyandanch, you know these slack-jaw WASP idiots off Exit 60 and beyond.

MIKE. I guess it is pretty dismal out there, all right.

CARL. So I'm waiting for the trains. I figure, fuck this, I can beat it. I punch the gas, the Eldorado jumps, and I go for it! This train hits me, man, throws the car like a fucking matchbox. I go to the hospital, broken ribs, shit's sprained, and my arms and legs are just fucked...and a bunch of other shit.

MIKE. Crazy, Dad. That's like a PSA for slowing down.

CARL. Ah, fuck all that. So a couple a days later, I hobble out of the hospital. I figure Long Island Railroad will pay me, compensate me for my troubles.

MIKE. Are you kidding? It was your fault.

CARL. Just listen, Michael! Jesus. So I go to the main office. Some expediter or superintendent. You know, one of these pension lifer assholes. Gives me a dirty look, like I'm the motherfucker who robbed the pony express.'

MIKE. I know exactly the type.

CARL. Sure you do, your mother's family is chock full of these scumbags.

MIKE. All right, come on Dad, take it easy. Nothing wrong with Mom's family.

CARL. Yeah mm hmm. So this fat mick cocksucker says, "Hey Jew boy, you the moron who tried to beat the train? You here for your little payout, you dumb fucking kike?"

MIKE. Jesus! Really? He said that?

CARL. Oh yeah, no political correct shit then. Some shanty Irish motherfucker from Far Rockaway. Some 9-to-5 cocksucker with a hard-on for anybody who doesn't buy into the same.

MIKE. Yeah, well, everybody's got his or her lot in life.

CARL. Yeah, well to me that's a vacant fucking lot! So the guys like, "Here's $800, asshole. Hit the road, hymie."

MIKE. Can't turn that down.

CARL. Hell no! Nineteen-and-sixty-fuckin'-eight, that's a lot of money! Plus the hospital bill was $750. Never paid 'em, I gave them an alias: "Donald Hall." That's the—

MIKE. ...Name on my birth certificate. It took years to figure that out. Created problems with my schooling, the DMV, trying to get a passport....

CARL. How do you think *I* felt? I had three different aliases going. Try juggling that!

Mike sighs.

LONG ISLAND CALLING!

My aunt is 75, and lives in Lake Ronkonkoma, New York. I called her after 20 years of non-com. After catching up with general family stuff—*Your uncle Kenny is too Jewish, with all the celebrating and his constant use of the Hebrew verbiage, it's like the second coming of the Talmud. Your Uncle Stevie is a recluse; he sits around writing the sports page for* New York Newsday *and just emails it in. Daddy and Mommy really damaged him, he never got a proper ass-whipping; he was the baby, you know*—she asked me about my father.

"He's got Alzheimer's and dementia," I told her.

"GOOD! FUCK HIM! I hope he's shitting all over himself, and talking to people who don't exist, you must still be so furious!"

"Nah, I don't care anymore, Aunt Bernice. I'm pretty neutral at this point." This incensed her.

"What? After all that scumbag did? Beat you kids! Married six times! He should die! He chiseled every cent out of every wife! Never gave your mom child support!" She paused to catch her breath. "How is your mother? You know we hung out in the Village and saw Miles Davis and John Coltrane. We even saw Judy Garland in Westbury, before she got all fucked up on pills and Vincent beat her. Or was that after that? Whatever, that's what I heard. But your father...forgetaboutit. *Oy gevalt*, like a *golem*. An absolute monster."

"Aunt Bernice, you know, that anger and rage will kill me. It kept me loaded on deadly amounts of drugs and alcohol. It made me felonious, and just plain psychotic. I've learned these things over the years in the program...."

"Well whatever. Program *shmogram*, he's still a fucking animal. You don't know the shit he put our family through, with all the lying, cheating, and stealing...always had to have the best of the best. Stole it if he couldn't afford it. A monster, Michael—just like your grandpa Samuel, another terror! You know he owned a couple of delicatessens in the Bronx, Queens, and Manhattan. Michael, he learned ways to fold the corn beef and pastrami—actually all the meats—in a specific way to make the sandwich appear much bigger. IT WORKED! But anybody that complained got escorted out quickly, with a swift kick in the ass. He would use red dye on the old meats, to make them appear fresh and new. I worked there for a couple of summers; you had to check with him before you threw anything out. When dine-in customers left a half-eaten sandwich, the meat went right back into the deli case. Leftover, even half-eaten pickles were turned into hot dog relish. I'm surprised he didn't rebottle leftover seltzers and sodas! The desserts, another story. He cut Danish and cakes so thin, like he was cutting bread for the needy...cheap asshole. And your grandmother, a pushover, she just settled with all his trickery and his frugal *fugazy* finagling bullshit."

We moved on to current events. She said there was no way she was getting a cell phone, that the price and the hidden fees were tremendous. Even the commercials annoyed the shit out of her.

"These advertisements, it's like nobody ever talked before these cockamamie phones. Now the whole fucking family is back together, just communicating and in love. What dreck. It's the opposite of that, trust me...."

She claimed the fine print in these so-called contracts

was designed exclusively by Jewish attorneys to fuck the common man (as well as Jews) out of their money. She also said that there are probably dangerous electrons or something toxic radiating out of them, going into your ears and rotting your brain, turning the nation even more apathetic. Thank G-d for Obamacare, because it's just a matter of time till there is a wave of serious brain damage and mental disabilities worse than there is now. And really, who the hell (except maybe a doctor) really needs a cellphone? "Who, Michael?"

I knew it was rhetorical, so I didn't answer.

She talked about television. She said it's basically gone to shit.

"460 out of the 468 channels I have are mindless drivel. These asshole B-list celebrities hocking their cheap made-in-China clothing and costume jewelry. And the food channel, with their greasy, thrice-fried hillbilly garbage...that one guy, eating food 'til he vomits.... That station hasn't been good since Emeril Agassi." She paused. "Then, even worse, these idiotic wives-of-sports-stars reality shows. Michael, it's no wonder why they get beaten. Reality TV! It's horrible! It'll leave a shit stain on the cultural fabric of America that will never ever come out!"

She called the Kardashians "dumb *shiksa* twats with fat asses, high heels and high drama." She stated they obviously had a penchant for porn, shock, and awe. "If they hadn't made a sex tape, they'd be belly dancing at a low-rent Middle Eastern restaurant. Or even worse, common street whores getting pimped by that ugly rum-blistered Bruce Jenner, who by the way is becoming a woman. He's *becoming a woman*, Michael! Those idiots really made him insane. He thinks he's one of them now! What a shame that man has become, he was on the Wheaties box! All those gold medals, look at him now, Michael. LOOK AT HIM NOW! The Kardashians! They're nobodies!" She yelled.

"The woman of my day were pure class. Sure, some were alcoholics and junkies (G-d rest Billie Holiday's soul) or deemed insane—Francis Farmer, I still love you. But they still had integrity. Women today.... Why, Michael? Why?"

Again, rhetorical.

"Annnd don't get me started with the news! It's a fucking horror show, chock full of refrigerator-white idiots who never had to struggle. These *goyim*, these blank-faced, shallow, slack-jaw idiots straight out of some cookie-cutter Ivy League university. They never challenge anything or anybody! They're like lemmings, just following the rest of the bewildered herd right off a g-ddamn man-made mountain of ignorance and stupidity."

I couldn't help but laugh and occasionally cheer her on through her tirade: *"Go, go!"*

She said she loved *Boardwalk Empire*, and even though Buscemi was an ugly little anorexic toad, he was talented nonetheless. The casting was perfect.

"It's way off-base historically, and at first it made the New York Jew gangsters look like soft *feygeles*. And that diminutive little homo that plays Capone? Come on, Michael, are you fucking kidding me? Alfonse must be spinning in his casket!"

She said she has no computer. "I don't email, I want to be heard, not read!" She loathed Facebook. "Michael, who gives a rat's ass where you went to dinner, or your hangnail, your cancer, or how you want to save the environment? Or the worst—pictures of your children. Why advertise for the pedophiles, for these internet sex predators who just sit around jerking off and eating delivery food, looking for a child to victimize?"

She said she sneaked a peek at my cousin's Facebook to see pictures of me. She said I looked very handsome and I should model, but not that homoerotic Herb Ritts shit. "You know, ties and jackets, jeans and Pendletons—rugged-man-type stuff."

Although "the *schvartze* Obama is a war-monger-
ing *gonnif*," she'll take him over "that *schnorrer* Romney"
any day. "G-d, what an idiot. He should take his magic
underwear, those psychotic-looking, date-raping sons, and
that stupid looking *shiksa* Stepford Wife, load 'em all into
a big sedan, and drive off a cliff. Take the poor dog off the
roof first, that should go without saying.

"Don't get me started with that putzy little douchebag
Paul Ryan. I think under it all he has a vagina, Michael.
I mean what's with his opinion, or *any* man's opinion for
that matter, on abortion? Why, Michael? Why? *Oy*, Ryan.
This schmuck has the look of a well-reared little tennis pro
who just walked off a whites-only country club. Believe me,
Michael, I'm sure in the comfort of his own home he prob-
ably doubts the massacre of a single Jew, and reads *Mein
Kampf* and Ayn Rand to form super-slogans that the Repub-
lican Tea Party can tout!"

She said most food was horrible these days. There were
only a couple of decent delis around New York now. The
goyim and Chinese fucked 'em all up, with their ridiculous
buffets and fusion-type food.

"I don't want Asian/Spanish-hybrid tiny food that
wouldn't fill a sparrow's belly. Michael, enough with the fu-
sion, how about some focus? It's often too dry, or too soggy.
And the pastries! It's like some jerkoff sits in a kitchen and
thinks of ways to make things with less flavor, less sugar.
HEY! The hell with your diabetes, don't punish me! Right,
Michael? This shitty swill they sell and call food, THE
NERVE! And, these brain-dead idiots of this new genera-
tion don't know any better.

"Well, I gotta take my afternoon nap, great talking to
you. For G_d's sake, stay off the freebase, and enough with
the drinking. That has to come from your Irish mother's
side, although I knew a lot of Jews that were cokeheads,
packing those schnozzes til they went cuckoo! So I guess

you got a little of both. I love you—please stay in touch!

"OK Aunt Bernice, good talking to you."

AFTERWORD:
SETTLED IN (WELL, SORT OF)

If you've read everything up to this point, you've taken a serious walk through my mental landscape. After getting sober in 2005, I got a divorce and tried to hold on to money that was all made illegally, dealing drugs and a bunch of other felonious activity that I really don't want to write or talk about right now. This is what I've been able to piece together so far.

These last few years have been challenging, and I've relapsed a couple of times. There was a time when I was completely dominated by my upbringing, ideas, and faulty-as-fuck belief systems. I had to rid my body and mind of these tales. I was cut, dyed, and galvanized by the events in most of these stories, a victim of a self-fulfilling prophecy created by resentment, fear, and a desperate need for revenge. The only way to freedom was to get it all on paper. I rode/wrote it out, and I no longer have to live it. The comedy I found in all this drama has saved me from overdosing, drinking myself to death, or succumbing to suicidal ideations. It may sound dramatic, but it's a fact.

My sister wasn't so fortunate. She overdosed and died on February 23, 2012. My mother has been clean and sober for 32 years and I hold NOTHING against her regarding my upbringing. The truth is, she had it FAR worse then I did. I still check out from time to time and fall into a morass of self-pity, bitterness, anger, and self-centeredness.

I've learned to turn to writing, performing, or just being a jackass across social media to quell (or at least quiet) those demons. I'm still fueled and possessed by a mild amount of evil and decay, which I am eternally grateful for. I stay spiritual by the daily admission that I'm not the least bit spiritual.

I'm just some ball of energy in a skin suit, navigating my way through an extremely broken world. A world filled with all the trappings that an addict like me could completely check the fuck out on. I did that already. I seriously dredged around the bottom of my soul with a selfie stick, looking for anything that resembled hope; it came up empty and totally overexposed. I used to find mediocrity mundane and boring, but now I see that it contains a plethora of information (albeit trite) that can be crafted into exquisite words. For me, not all of the observational subject matter has to be hip, slick, and glossy in order to shine at another level.

It's like this: I built it up and burned it down so many times. I ventured into Southeast Asia stone-cold sober and hit bottoms (pardon the pun) with sexual behavior that turned my stomach and churned my soul. I walked aimlessly for hours on the streets of Los Angeles pondering my foul existence and the complete and utter damage I created and dealt in the form of love, drugs, violence, and manipulation. I felt that raw rub of burning everything out between me and me, me and you, and me and fucking everyone. I sat quietly with monks at Angkor Wat and never felt so tragically guilty and unworthy, and woke up to the vicious selfishness that engulfs my very twisted First-World being. And I realized it was all gonna be OK. I had money, lots of money, but never felt as secure as I do now with so little. Now I'm so filled with self-respect, love, and a wife and extended family that has taken me in, craziness and all.

At times I say and do ridiculously stupid and immature things. I see the areas of my life where my thinking is small, microscopically small; that place where no love, no patience or tolerance lives. And I realize that my ego, my need to be right, has made me a punk in the prison of my own mind. I was lucky enough to find an improv class (Upright Citizens Brigade) and I stayed with that group of people for years. I learned to listen, observe, and play with my words. During that run, I got to get on stage with Robin Williams and learned to shut up and let the master speak—then I got to shine, too.

I've had a love-hate relationship with 12-step meetings since 1982. Ah, meetings! *(Time to rant....)* Meetings filled with grifters, hustlers, poseurs, producers, actors, agents, writers, directors, rockers, and phony doctors. Then there are the money-grabbers, liars, cheaters, thieves, and bikers. Also, gear-heads, surfers, sexual predators, 60-year-old punkers, and second-story men. Bad teeth, bad caps, stupid hats, dirty, unwashed, smelly asses; silicone tits, cheeks, and butts. Chrome hearts, gurus, yoga teachers, and spiritual make-believers. Faith-based shitfaced hillbillies and city slickers, age-inappropriate fashion disasters, bad hair, bad vibes, and a constant barrage of unwanted hugs and touching. And I love it all, the microcosm of the country, under one roof.

But in all seriousness, within that highly diversified circus of human beings, I met some incredible people who understood where I came from, and helped me immensely to get through my upbringing, shaping me into the person I am now. I've been given a new opportunity to face the person that I thought I was, and actually become someone that I didn't even know I wanted to be—allowing me to access these stories and to give you this book through the clear eyes of the authenticity that self-introspection has afforded me.

ACKNOWLEDGMENTS

First and foremost, I want to thank my mother, and my hero, Mary Agnes Lydon. My sister Lorraine (RIP), who raised me in the midst of a virtual fucking latchkey hell. I want to thank Bill and Bob. I want to thank and always acknowledge my beautiful wife Dana, who has stuck by me through all of it, and never gave up on me. My in-laws—I love you. My father, Carl Marcus (RIP)—you did the best you could with what you had. My stepfather, Daniel Faigenbaum (RIP), Iris Berry, Wyatt Doyle, Punk Hostage Press and all the badass writers in that crew. Marc Maron, Jerry Stahl, Malcolm Venville, Max Silver, Jon Hess, Jack Grisham, Andrew "Razor" Lopas, Walter Bruan & the whole Bruan clan, Dylan Mullick, JB Bogulski, Pat Ridge, and Roy Tighe. I want to acknowledge The Upright Citizen's Brigade, The Moth, all the crazy women, junkies, thieves, intellectuals, artists, poets, punk rockers, hippies, metal heads, rappers, investors, criminals, graffiti artists, anti-social psychotic characters, geeks and freaks and chumps and hustlers. You shaped me and made me what I am today.

MICHAEL MARCUS currently lives in the erstwhile barrio of Glassel Park, along with his wonderful wife and two aging cats. He was born in Freeport, Long Island, or as he likes to call it, Cirrhosis by the Sea. His Irish-Catholic mother comes from Far Rockaway, New York—The Irish Riviera. His Romanian-Jewish father hails from The Bronx. Growing up, he never felt he fit in anywhere, and has tried his hand at many jobs—legal, and not so much. Reading, writing, and performing saw him through the literal trauma and hell he grew up in. This collection of stories reflects those memories. There is more to come.

ALSO FROM PUNK HOSTAGE PRESS

When I Was a Dynamiter, or, How a Nice Catholic Boy
Became a Merry Prankster, a Pornographer, and a
Bridegroom Seven Times by Lee Quarnstrom

Introvert/Extrovert by Russell Jaffe

No Greater Love by Die Dragonetti

No Parachutes to Carry Me Home by Maisha Z Johnson

By Jack Grisham
Untamed
Code Blue: A Love Story

By Alexandra Naughton
I Will Always Be Your Whore/Love Songs for
Billy Corgan
You Could Never Objectify Me More Than I've Already
Objectified Myself

By A. Razor
Better Than a Gun in a Knife Fight
Drawn Blood: Collected Works From D.B.P. Ltd.,
1985-1995
Beaten Up Beaten Down
Small Catastrophes in a Big World
Half-Century Status
Days of Xmas Poems

CPSIA information can be obtained
at www.ICGtesting.com
Printed in the USA
BVOW08s1140070118

504654BV00001B/254/P